# More Meanderings from Doc's Diary

by

Charles Lamb

*Benson Smythe Publishing*
*Wellsville, New York*

**More Meanderings from Doc's Diary**
ISBN 1-888911-18-2
Library of Congress Number
99-075759

10 9 8 7 6 5 4 3 2 1

To order this book write to:
Benson Smythe Publishing
3052 Palmer Road
Wellsville, New York 14895-9746
or call
716-593-6145

Published by Benson Smythe Publishing
3052 Palmer Road
Wellsville, New York 14895-9746

*Cover and book design by*
*Christina Case Wightman*

Printed in the United States by
Morris Publishing
3212 East Highway 30
Kearney, NE 68847
1-800-650-7888

To my delight, many people have told me that they received great pleasure from reading my previous book, *Doc's Diary*. One person said, "I laughed out loud, and had to keep reading until I finished it." Another remarked, "My downstairs neighbor heard me laughing!"

Different stories appealed to different people. One would comment on "Blue Shoes in Heaven" while another would mention "Keep on Truckin." Probably the one that drew the most comments was "Lord, Let Me Be Anywhere But Here."

I was especially pleased to learn that church groups had used some of the stories for studies or devotionals. I had hoped that the stories would not only be amusing but also inspirational. I know that at least "The Early Christmas Gift" and "Angel Really Is One" were used in this way.

Many have asked me, "When are you going to do a sequel?" The answer to that is, "Now!" After 28 years in regional ministry, I have an abundance of material for these tales.

A regional minister is just what the name implies; that is, a minister who works not only with one congregation but with all the churches in a region. In the Northeastern Region of the Christian Church (Disciples of Christ), where I served from 1971 through 1998, many of our congregations are Hispanic, Haitian, or African American, as well as Anglo. Some are rural; some are urban. They are located from the upper shores of Maine to the southwestern corner of New York State, including New York City and New Jersey. This means that there are very different settings, and people, to meet.

I have changed the names of people and places and sometimes combined incidents, but these stories are all based on fact. If anyone feels that they recognize themselves, I hope they will be assured that any laughter is directed not at them, but with them, and any ridicule is aimed only at myself.

I have divided the stories in this volume into three sections. The first is entitled "Experiences Extraordinary," and is written much in the manner of the stories in "Doc's Diary." I wish to share with the readers some noteworthy encounters I have had with some remarkable individuals as I went along the way.

In the second section, "Hospital Horrors and Hallelujahs," I relate a number of incidents that took place while I was hospitalized for a long period. A difficult-to-diagnose fungus had taken up residence in my anklebone following a bad break, and I was released from the hospital only after 8 operations and 4 months of being a hostage. I won't dwell on the pain, just the people, and hope that any who face hospital ordeals may find that they can relate very well to some of these stories. Even in illness, laughter can help one endure.

Romans 8:28, in older versions of the Bible, states that "...all things work together for good to them that love God..." Some newer versions say instead, "...in everything God works for good with those who love him...." Greek scholars tell me that either translation is possible, based on the text. The latter one certainly seems more believable to me! I felt about my hospital ordeal much like some tell me they felt about basic military training: "I'm glad I had the experience but I wouldn't want to do it again." I had some good experiences I would never have had otherwise, and met some amazing people as my roommates came and went, and that is what I want to share.

In the final section of these "Meanderings," entitled "The Wisdom of Walter," I hope to show how there is sometimes more thought-provoking thoughts that come from the lips of a little child than are to be found from the pens of the learned. Funny and unexpected observations set me to thinking later, and I think those who read these stories may have the same reaction.

I am grateful to have found an editor and publisher, Christina Wightman, who believes in the value of my writing and shares with me the conviction that laughter and inspiration are good companions. My hope is that the readers of *More Meanderings From Doc's Diary* will come to the same conclusion.

# Table of Contents

## *Experiences Extraordinary*

## *Hospital Horrors and Hallelujahs*

# Experiences
# Extraordinary

## *Spending the Night at Brother Bob's*

Brother Bob was the holiest man in any of our churches! At least he gave that appearance. As I headed down the highway to his church and home, I wondered if the piety would overwhelm me.

When Brother Bob, as he liked to be called, had first come to Pinesville Christian Church I was quite worried. Pinesville had gone outside our ministerial search system and found Brother Bob on their own. He had no credentials in our denomination. Furthermore, he was from a more charismatic type church than ours, which took the Bible very literally, believed in speaking in tongues, and in general, considered people like me to be "worldly". I feared it would be just a short time until he tried to take the church out of the denomination.

My fears were unjustified. Brother Bob, although he had his own beliefs, tried to cooperate with us fully. He attended district meetings, promoted our special offerings, and announced our news. He sometimes invited me to preach. Although there was no doubt about his own convictions, nor that he preached them, he did so in a non-judgmental way that was acceptable. I began to relax and feel that maybe this little rural church was in good hands after all.

I thought Brother Bob's admonitions against not only

drinking and smoking but also against movies, makeup, shorts, or swimming coed would get him into a lot of trouble with the congregation, but they seemed to like him pretty well. I know many of his members didn't agree with what he said, but the man had a winsome personality, and he was always there for a person in trouble. He visited the sick, played with the young people, listened to people's problems, and generally radiated love and concern. Since we Disciples of Christ allow people the right to differences of opinion, I guess the congregation extended the same right to their minister.

I was going to spend Saturday night at Brother Bob's and his wife Martha's house and then preach for him on Sunday morning. I arrived at the parsonage, which stood next door to the church, around 9:00 p.m. I knew there would be no glass of wine for the weary traveler, but I wasn't expecting the full-blown Bible study class that was waiting for me!

Brother Bob and Martha greeted me at the door and then ushered me inside their attractive living room. There were crocheted doilies on the tables and pictures of Jesus on the walls. A large Bible was open on the coffee table. The stereo was playing Gospel music. After taking my suitcase and placing it aside, Brother Bob clasped both my hands and said, "May God bless you, my brother, for coming to this home where Jesus is the host and we all are his guests."

"Amen, and er, uh, thank you," I replied.

Sister Martha was bringing me a King James Bible and showing me where to sit down. "It's almost bedtime," she cooed, "but you're here in time for our evening devotions."

Brother Bob explained that they discussed a scripture each evening, and since he read from the King James version maybe I could use their's tonight. He knew I usually used a more modern translation. Of course I agreed and settled myself down for what turned out to be a rather prolonged discussion of the Beatitudes from Matthew chapter five. Brother Bob's commentary was all right as far as I was concerned; I just didn't know I was coming to a Bible class that night until I was already into it.

After half an hour or so of the lesson, Brother Bob evidently decided that all three of us had received enough admonitions and exhortations for one evening, so he said we could stand, hold hands, and close with prayer. He prayed for me long and loud, thanking God for my visit, my ministry, and my life. I thought for a minute he was just trying to impress me but when I peeked at his face, his sincere and loving expression made me feel otherwise. "This man is really a saint," I thought. "Even though I'm not used to so much piety, I have to respect him for it."

After the prayer, Brother Bob said he would show me to my bedroom which was up the stairs. I picked up my suitcase and followed him. As we ascended, he explained that his son was away in college so I would be in his bedroom for the evening.

We came to the top of the stairs and Brother Bob opened his son's bedroom door, and I stepped into another world! I gasped in amazement! The walls were all plastered with pin-up pictures! Heather Locklear gazed down from the ceiling, over the bed! I had not seen so much female flesh in such provocative poses in magazine stores as I found in this bedroom! I was in the midst of a nest of eroticism!

Brother Bob caught my look of amazement, and immediately began to apologize. "Oh, Doc," he said, "I should have thought about it. You see, my son isn't saved yet; he's pretty worldly. He is twenty years old and this is his room. I don't try to control what he puts in here. I don't condone it, mind you. If it offends you I can offer you another place to sleep."

By now I was recovering my equilibrium, and I laughed out loud. "Oh no, Brother Bob! I'll stay here! In fact, I'll probably leave the lights on all night long!"

Did I really say that? Sometimes, when amused, I speak without thinking of my audience!

Now it was his turn to look amazed! Did the Regional Minister really like this sort of thing?

"Brother Bob," I said, "you continue to amaze me. You have such strong religious convictions, but you don't try to impose them on others. You let your son live his own life; you influence him but you don't demand that he conform to your views. I think he's a lucky son to have you as a father, and Martha as a mother."

Brother Bob looked a bit reassured and wished me a good night. I wonder if he got up later to look at the crack under my door to see if I really did leave the lights on all night!

# 2

## *The Best Christmas Gift*

This year I was going all out! Betty loves to watch birds, especially hawks, so I was sure she'd really be thrilled to get a pair of binoculars for Christmas! Then she could carry them in the car and when she spotted a hawk she could pull to the side of the road, take out her binoculars, and get a good look!

It amused me that she liked hawks so much. After all they are a vicious kind of bird, soaring aloft until they can swoop down on an unsuspecting rabbit or squirrel or mourning dove. Betty is a kind person; it seemed out of character for her to be a hawk lover.

I don't think she thought about the hunting so much. She just admired the hawk's beauty as it soared aloft in graceful circles in the sky or perched at the very tip-top of the tallest tree. She often remarked, "Oh, Doc, look at that hawk! Isn't it a beauty?" So we would stop the car and look. However, you can't see too much with the unaided eye from a long distance, and that is why I thought binoculars would be the best Christmas gift I could give her. I knew she would be so surprised and happy, and that would make me happy too.

I was in for a shock when I arrived at the store and began to look at the selection. I ruled out the large ones. They would be too bulky for her to carry very conveniently. I also didn't want the little opera glasses. I wanted a compact, but powerful, pair that would give a clear view from a long distance yet small and easy to manage.

The store certainly had binoculars that fit that description, but at what a price! I had no idea! $250! I had expected $75 or $100 at most. I wasn't prepared for the larger price.

But, what the heck! It was almost Christmas. She deserved the best, and she would have them forever. It was easy to talk myself into being extravagant, especially since they had an easy-payment plan!

So I got the binoculars, wrapped them, put them under our tree, and felt more anticipation for Betty's reaction when she opened her gift than I did for anything I might be receiving. After all, I remembered, "It is more blessed to give than to receive."

As Christmas drew near, our house was bustling with anticipation. Two of our daughters were coming with their children. Our two sons would also be there. There were four grandchildren coming too! Betty was busy planning the meal and making sure everyone's presents were wrapped and that there was approximately the same number of gifts for each grandchild! Children seem to notice these things, and it is hard for little ones to understand that one gift may cost as much as three others. We always do too much for Christmas!

On the 23rd, Betty seemed thoughtful when I arrived home. "Doc," she said, "I just found out that Irma, from our church, is planning to spend Christmas day alone. That bothers me."

Irma was an elderly lady who belonged to our church. I knew she had two children, but both lived far away (near the west coast). I would have assumed that at least one of them would have come, had I thought about it. Evidently neither one was coming.

"Doc, I can hardly bear to think of her spending Christmas day all alone in that big house!" Betty continued. "She is a sweet lady, and she deserves better. One more person

**6**

won't hurt. Why don't we invite her to share Christmas with us?"

I admired Betty's generosity, and I liked Irma too, but I knew our house would be filled with pandemonium with all the kids and grandkids there. I wasn't sure if a quiet lady like Irma would like that.

"Do you really think that's a good idea?" I asked. "Wouldn't she rather be with someone her age? I mean, she is quiet and she has other friends." I really felt pretty reluctant about it.

"Other friends have families, and other plans, I guess," Betty responded. "All I know is that our minister told me that Irma is going to be alone. I think we should do something about it."

"Well," I replied, "I guess we could ask her. She'll probably say 'No' but she'll know she was invited."

That was all the encouragement Betty needed. She wheeled around and picked up the phone, dialed Irma's number, and enthusiastically invited Irma to come have Christmas at our house!

I could hear only Betty's end of the conversation, of course, but after hearing her repeatedly reassuring Irma that "No, you won't be any trouble at all" and "Of course we'll come pick you up!" and "Yes, we're sure we really want you," she turned from the phone smiling broadly. "She's coming, Doc!"

I was glad Betty was happy but slightly concerned how it would all work out and a little worried that one of us would have to drive to get her. If Betty went, I wasn't sure I was ready to be host for four grandchildren climbing all over me by myself!

I soon put these thoughts out of my mind, however. There was too much to do: last minute shopping, decorations we had neglected to put out, quick trips to the grocery store for indispensable items Betty needed as she prepared food. Right up until dark on Christmas Eve, we were busy!

7

We had a beautiful candlelight service, with Communion, at our church on Christmas Eve. The minister spoke about the gift of God's Son and the gift of God's love. She said that this should motivate us to give too, and reminded us that there was more joy in giving than in receiving. I knew that. I thought immediately of the binoculars, cleverly boxed so their shape wouldn't be obvious, waiting under the tree for Betty's joyful discovery on Christmas morning.

Christmas Day dawned bright, crisp, and beautiful. The sun made the snow-covered trees sparkle. It was one of those magic moments. We woke up and enjoyed the day, waiting to open presents until all of the company arrived. We were planning a brunch at 2:00 so our daughters' children could see what Santa brought them in their own homes before bundling up and coming to our house for dinner and more presents.

As we lay there, anticipating the day, the phone rang. Betty answered; it was Irma. She had come down with a nasty cold. She felt miserable and couldn't come. She didn't feel up to it, and besides, she couldn't spread her germs to a whole house full of people. She was grateful for the invitation, but no, she really needed to stay home.

Betty was sad. I was a bit relieved! I was sorry for Irma too, but also knew now Betty would be home to help me with the host duties all day long, and I wouldn't have to worry about excited, happy, but noisy children getting on our guest's nerves.

I noticed Betty was a bit subdued as she finished preparations for dinner. Of course she brightened up as soon as the company arrived! With squeals of joy, the grandchildren rushed toward the tree and had to be restrained from opening one another's presents. It is so hard for a child who is five to hold back and allow a child who is two to open her own gifts! "I just want to help!"

It was fun. There is nothing like the excitement in a child's face to make the adults happy too.

When Betty opened her binoculars, the moment I had been waiting for, her reaction exceeded my fondest hopes. She was obviously surprised. I could see from her expression she was very pleased, and she threw her arms around my neck and kissed me on the cheek before she remembered to say, "Doc, are you sure we can afford this?"

When I said we could she answered in typical Betty fashion by deciding that of course I must use them too and that I should not give her anything else when her birthday came; this was too much! But I knew she liked them.

All in all, everyone, including me, had a good time and seemed happy with the gifts chosen for them. Of course some of the children's gifts had to be assembled, but that's what their parents were for! Not my job anymore! I hate those things with 100 pieces and the instructions that say "So simple a child can assemble" which I either break or abandon in frustration after an hour of trying!

I had a beautiful robe; I needed one for my travels. I could jump up and go to the bathroom in my pajamas at home, but on the road I had to be a little more proper when I went down the hall in the middle of the night. If I ever blundered into the wrong room again, at least I'd be conservatively dressed!

Dinner was delicious; there was ham and potatoes and squash and green beans and fruit salad and at least a dozen other dishes. Even our son who is a chef assured his mom that she had done a quality job.

After dessert, we were ready to relax, let the children play with their new treasures, and just enjoy one another's company. Betty was happy but somehow I could tell she was not quite as involved in the festivities as usual. Suddenly she said, "I've got to excuse myself for about an hour. You all just enjoy yourselves." She jumped up and stared filling another plate.

"What are you doing?" I asked. "Where are you going?" I couldn't imagine!

"I just can't stand it another minute, Doc," she said, "to think of Irma over there in her house all alone and sick. Maybe she's feeling well enough to eat something. I'm going to take her a Christmas dinner."

That was nice, I was sure. I hadn't thought of such a thing. "But Betty, maybe she's sick in bed?"

"Well, maybe she is; then she can put it in the refrigerator. But maybe she's hungry. Anyhow, she'll know somebody is thinking of her and wishing her a merry Christmas!"

This was just like Betty; I had to admire it. "Okay," I said, "but *please* hurry back!"

Our daughters pitched in to wash the dishes, and the men helped off and on drying them and putting them away. At least they did until the women told them just to go watch the football game and get out of the way!

Pretty soon Betty came home, with her face flushed from the cold and a happy sparkle in her eyes. "Doc," she said, "I'm so glad I did that! Irma met me at the door and she was so surprised. She kept saying, 'You didn't have to do this!' and I kept saying 'I know that; I wanted to do it!' Doc, her eyes flooded with tears; I could see it was just exactly the right thing for me to have done. She said, 'I'll never forget this, Betty!' I feel like we gave her Christmas after all!"

Betty was using the term "we" generously. I hadn't thought of inviting her. I hadn't cooked the meal. I hadn't delivered it. In fact, I'd spoken hesitantly about it. But Betty said "we" had given Irma Christmas. I told her I could take no credit.

"Yes you can, Doc! You agreed for me to invite her, you agreed for me to go without making a fuss, and you did all the dishes while I was gone!"

Actually, our children had done the dishes; oh well, let that pass!

So the day ended on a happy note. Our kids took their tired children home; soon all was quiet. Betty and I scrambled about, picking up discarded wrapping paper, taking the leaves out of the dining room table, generally putting the house back in order. We sat down for a sandwich of leftover ham, talked about the day, and decided it was bedtime early. We were both exhausted, but happy.

**10**

After climbing into bed Betty lay in my arms and we talked for a few minutes before going to sleep. Somehow I couldn't resist asking her one question.

"Betty," I said, "it was a wonderful Christmas. But tell me, what was the very best part of Christmas this year?"

I knew what she would say. The binoculars, of course! I had spent a fortune, and I could see in her eyes when she opened them how thrilled she was. She had already thanked me; I guess I just wanted to hear it one more time.

"Oh, Doc," she said. "So many good things happened! How can I mention one?"

I knew she was just teasing me, as she sometimes does. Of course many good things happened, but not in the league with the binoculars! "Come on, Betty! If only one thing had happened to you to make you happy today, what would it have been? What thrilled you the most?"

I waited for my strokes, my moment of affirmation.

"You really want to know, Doc?"

"I sure do!"

"It was taking dinner to Irma! That was the highlight of my day, the part of this Christmas I'll always remember!"

"Oh!"

"Doc, what's the matter?"

"Nothing at all," I said. "Let me tell you the highlight of this Christmas for me. It's being married to you; learning all over again what Christmas is all about. It's more blessed to give than to receive. I guess you just illustrated that all over again."

"You always knew that, Doc," she said. "You're a minister."

"But sometimes," I said, "I forget."

11

# 3

## *The Day I Had AIDS*

During my stay in the hospital, with its multiple operations (related later in this book), I had to have a lot of blood
transfusions. I had told the doctor I'd rather not, but he said the
operations could not wait, and I had to have more blood. So,
with trepidation, I agreed.

The fear of AIDS was strong in our society and in me.
Despite the assurances of the hospital that the blood was
screened and that it was far less likely that AIDS would be in
the blood than hepatitis, I still worried.

Sometime after coming home, I decided to make a
change in our life insurance policies. My insurance man wanted to shift my coverage from one company, whose financial
position had become a bit precarious, to another one that he
thought was more stable. I agreed, and it turned out that he was
right; the first company went into bankruptcy a couple of years
later.

A nurse phoned me; she worked for the new insurance
company. She needed to come to my house and take a blood
test. That was a routine requirement by her company, she
explained.

Of course I agreed. When she arrived she asked me to
sign a statement that they could test my blood for AIDS.
"Sure!" I said. "I'll be so reassured to know that I don't have

AIDS."

Then I asked, "What is the procedure? Do you contact me to tell me that I do or don't and that my insurance is or is not approved?"

"Well," she said, "if your blood is fine, you won't hear anything. In a few weeks you'll get your new policy in the mail."

"But if by any chance I did have AIDS, what then?" I asked.

"You would be notified," she said. "We'd send a letter directly to you, advising you to see your physician."

"When would I know?" I continued.

She smiled. I guess she sensed that I was nervous. "I'm sure you're fine," she said. "But if there was anything wrong, you'd get a letter in about two weeks."

Every day of the following two weeks I was determined not to think about it, but thought about little else. "It will feel so good," I said to myself, "just to know for sure that the doctors were right and all that blood I received in the hospital was okay."

Two weeks to the day after my blood test, I came home to find in our mail box a notice that a piece of registered mail was waiting for me at the post office. Since I was not at home when the postman came, it had been carried back to the post office to await my signing for it.

I backed out of the driveway immediately and raced to the post office. It had just closed.

I was sure what the mail was going to be. "Of course they wouldn't send out a notice of something as serious as AIDS by regular mail," I told myself. "They would send it by registered mail. And there is nothing else that I am expecting. It is exactly two weeks today since my test!"

At first I thought it *might* mean I had AIDS. Within an hour I had no doubt. By 8:00 p.m. I was a basket case.

"Betty," I said, "I've been with people who had AIDS and who have died of it. I am not going to go through that nor

**13**

put you through that. I just can't."

Betty urged me just to pray and relax and wait until morning. I prayed all right! But my prayers weren't the prayers of submission that bring peace, I must confess. They alternated between begging for healing and asking for courage.

For a long time I have thought that euthanasia is acceptable in certain cases, and not a sin. My theology calls for responsible decision making; I think God gives us that ability. After prayer, and hopefully in line with God's will, we make decisions all our life. We determine who to marry, what career to follow, when to have children and how many, etc. To determine to end a life of suffering seemed in line with that overall philosophy to me.

I had known one of our ministers, some years ago, who had been in a terminal health situation and decided to refuse all further treatment. "I'll be gone in a week," he told me, "so I'm glad you came to see me. The doctors say they can keep me comfortable. I'm tired of the constant treatments; it is time to go. My wife brings in the photograph albums and we look at them and remember and treasure our memories. I'd rather end it this way." His wife, at his side, smiled her agreement. In a week, as he predicted, he was gone.

That seemed like a responsible decision to me. Active intervention to end a life of prolonged and hopeless suffering seemed to me to be a responsible decision also. To have the ability and to decide not to use it is still a decision. God won't allow us to pass the buck; when God gives us life he gives us choice!

"But I won't do it right away, Betty," I assured her. "Only when it really gets bad."

I didn't sleep much that night. When the post office opened at 8:30 the next morning I was the first person into the lobby. I might as well get the bad news over.

And there it was, my diploma for my Doctor of Ministry degree. I hadn't gone to the commencement services so they mailed it to me! I had forgotten that it might be coming in the mail.

A few weeks later the life insurance policy arrived.

But for one night of my life, I had AIDS. I know the fear, the misery, the hopelessness, and the dismay that I felt, and I have more sympathy than ever before for those who really have AIDS.

I pray for God's comfort for them, for more bravery than I had, and for a cure!

I also pray that in the future I won't jump to conclusions quite so rapidly!

# 4

## *The Exploiters*

He was the most prosperous looking Haitian I had met so far during my trip to Haiti. "Portly" and "pompous" are the right adjectives to describe him, I thought, as I looked at him. He was a man that I estimated to be about 35 years old, dressed in a navy blue pin stripe suit with a vest. He was seated at the table next to me in the little side-street cafe. Since I noticed he was reading the New York Times, I decided to risk a conversation in English. "Are you from New York?" I asked.

"Why, yes I am," he said, "and are you also?"

Since he was willing to talk, I was glad to move ahead with the conversation. I told him that I was indeed from New York and was in Haiti visiting churches.

This definitely increased his interest. "Why?" he asked.

"My Haitian friend, who will be joining me in a moment, is a pastor in the New York area, but he has many contacts here. We are going to visit some of the churches with which he has a relationship. Maybe we can find ways to help them and have more contacts with them."

"You may be just the person I am looking for," he said. "I'm here to employ about fifty people. Maybe you can help me find them."

What a Godsend! If we could go to the churches with jobs to offer, then Matthew and I would bring very concrete

**16**

help to the people here.

At that moment Matthew came in and found us, and I excitedly introduced him to my new friend. Mr. Pierre squeezed out of the booth and stood to pump Matthew's hand vigorously and then eased back into his seat. "As I was saying to your friend here," he related to Matthew, "I'm planning to hire a number of people during my visit to Haiti. Since you are visiting churches, you may want to put some of the women in those churches in touch with me. I can offer them jobs."

"Isn't this good news, Matthew?" I exclaimed. Then turning to Mr. Pierre, I asked, "How is it that you can make such an offer?"

"Well," he said, with a smug smile, "it is because I am a good businessman. I learned that one of the chain department stores in the U.S. has the embroidery on its fancy towels done in the Philippines. All that is required is to put some decorative stitching around the edges of each towel; it can easily be done by any woman who can sew. I asked the retailer how much they paid their Philippine workers for the embroidery work. They told me $7.00 per day. So I told them, 'I can get it done for you for half that amount!' They gave me the contract. And now I've come to Haiti to find fifty people to do the work for $3.50 American money per day."

I felt myself becoming troubled. $3.50 a day! That seemed incredibly little to me. So I asked, "Mr. Pierre, I am not very familiar with the economy here yet, but that seems to me to be a very small amount to pay. Can a person here live on $3.50 a day?"

He laughed, as though I had just said something quite amusing. "Of course not!" he chuckled. "At least not like you and I want to live! They won't eat three meals, that's for sure! But they'll do it; they don't have any other offers!"

I felt myself becoming angry; that hot feeling that courses through your blood and makes you want to jump to your feet and react physically. I tried to control that inner heat, and to keep my voice calm. "You realize, of course, you're exploiting

**17**

your own people, don't you?"

Mr. Pierre reacted as though I had slapped him. He visibly recoiled. "Hey, man!" he responded. "I don't make the rules! That's the way the game is played!"

"Well, I don't play that way," I answered. "I want nothing to do with you or that kind of an offer."

He looked at me sulkily, and muttered, "$3.50 a day is better than the nothing they are getting now!" Then he glanced at Matthew to see how he was reacting. To my surprise, Matthew hadn't said anything during the exchange. I thought he would be angrier than I was. Probably because of Matthew's silence, Mr. Pierre began ignoring me and talking to him. He shoved a business card across the table and said, "If you change your mind, here's the way to contact me." We lapsed into silence; in a few moments Mr. Pierre rose from his seat, paid his bill, and left, glancing at me through lowered brows. I had made an enemy by calling him what he was. "Can you believe it, Matthew?" I exclaimed. "That man is a Haitian; he is one of the people from this country, but he is worse than a foreigner. He is taking advantage of the poverty of the people to make himself into a fat pig! And he has no shame nor sympathy for his kinsmen here at all. I am so disgusted."

Matthew replied in a quiet voice, "Doc, of course he is. It is really a shame. But you know, he's right about $3.50 a day being better than nothing at all. Most people here have no income and they'd be glad for anything."

"But Matthew," I argued, "we can't be part of such a rip-off! We'd be collaborating in cheating the people! The Church can't condone such a policy!"

"I know how you feel, Doc," Matthew said, "and I appreciate your concern for the people. But sometimes when you get a job, then later you can get a raise. We don't have anything better to offer, do we?"

And of course we didn't. I said, "Well, we'll have to figure something out."

I'm not sure, but I strongly suspect that Matthew later

contacted Mr. Pierre and put him in touch with some local con-gregations. If he did, I don't want to know it. Matthew is a practical man, and I can't judge him if that was his decision. I know how much he wants to help the people.

Leaving the cafe, we drove down the rutted street past stacks of garbage. I saw many people who were walking along or lounging in doorways. Some of the women, with beautiful posture, carried baskets balanced perfectly on their heads. I admired them for their poise.

I also saw a lot of goats! Many people seemed to have them, and they looked healthy enough. It was good to know that goats could live even in the midst of garbage and provide milk and sometimes meat for the people. I commented. "They're from Heifer Project, Doc," Matthew explained. I had always been a supporter of Heifer Project because that organi-zation's philosophy of sending cows, rabbits, chickens, or goats to people rather than just food made sense to me. The gift just kept on giving! It was good to know some people were not exploiters!

That night, back at the hotel, we parked the car and sat out on the patio in some folding chairs. The Haitian climate is wonderful. It was just warm enough to be comfortable, and a mild tropical breeze was moving through the palm trees. Soon we were joined by some other Americans who sat down nearby and began a conversation. When they learned that we were with the church, they said they were also. "We're missionaries too!" a young woman exclaimed.

I didn't think of us so much as missionaries as I did as just visiting fellow Christians, but I accepted the designation. She asked what we had been doing, and I explained that we were visiting churches to see how we could help them. I told her about my disappointment with the Haitian businessman.

She didn't seem too interested and didn't say anything to let me think she shared my indignation. "We're not into that kind of thing," she said, "like offering jobs. We're just here to preach the Gospel and save souls."

"Really?" I answered. "We are visiting about forty churches here; it seems to me there are churches on every street. I think the local pastors can do a better job of preaching than I can, especially since they speak Creole. We hope we can offer some fellowship with Christians back home and some practical help."

"Listen," she told me, "if these people get the Holy Spirit they won't need any material help. God will give them prosperity and abundance once they have the baptism of the Spirit."

I wasn't prepared for that kind of a remark! "Wait a minute," I urged. "Don't you know Jesus said that if we fed the hungry and clothed the naked, we had done it unto him? I've met some beautiful Christian people who love God, and if we love them too we'll want to share. They are in a terrible economic situation here due to the exploiting dictatorships under which they've suffered, and if we're their brothers and sisters we'll give them some help. What good does it do to talk to them about love if all we do is talk?"

"I suppose it is good if you want to do that kind of thing," she said, "but that isn't our calling. We're called to save their souls."

I began to wonder whose souls needed saving. Imagine, prosperous Americans coming to destitute Haiti and preaching, through translation, to people who were already Christian that their poverty was because they hadn't received God's Spirit!

She was still talking as my thoughts raced. "Sometimes Brother Bill preaches and sometimes Brother Don. Then we take up an offering and I sing."

I reacted with amazement. "You take up an offering?" I said. "From these people?"

"Why, of course!" she answered. "They feel more a part of it if they give some money."

The indignation I had felt against Mr. Pierre came back again, stronger than ever. These missionaries were not only exploiting the people, they were oblivious to the harm they

**20**

were doing. I hoped no Haitian really believed that poverty was a punishment from God and that prosperity would come if they donated to this crew.

"I hope you can visit some of our Haitian churches," I said, as I got up to walk away, ". . . and that you will let the pastors preach to you."

What a terrible day! I knew that the government of Haiti had exploited its people, draining the country of its resources and pocketing the money, but I wasn't prepared for Haitian businessmen and American missionaries to be doing the same!

But the day ended on a brighter note. Matthew and I were sitting on the patio again, just before bedtime, having a cup of coffee when the manager of the hotel joined us. We fell into a relaxed conversation. Although he wasn't a churchman, I felt more at ease with him than with the missionaries.

"Haiti has everything a country could need," he said. "We have the weather, the scenery, and beautiful friendly people. But tourists don't come here anymore because of the terrible government. No tourist agency advertises Haiti. I only survive from two sources: Haitians coming home to visit and religious people like you."

He paused suddenly and looked at Matthew and me strangely. "I hope you don't mind my saying so," he continued, "but you two seem different from those other missionaries."

"How so?" I asked. I certainly hoped so!

"Well, they just talk and talk and talk at me and never listen to anybody. I notice Haitian people coming here to meet you, and they talk to you. You two mostly listen."

"Thanks so much for noticing," I said. "That's what we're trying to do."

**5**

## *One Way to Handle the Situation*

It was time for the final hymn, but the minister waited in vain for the music to begin. Glancing at the organ, he noted that Hiram was not there. "Oh no, not again!" he muttered under his breath. Then he cleared his throat and tried to hit the right note to start the singing. "A song leader I'm not," he thought, "but we've got to muddle through this to get to the benediction."

Members of the congregation were grinning; they knew exactly what had happened. Hiram had his own way of showing his disapproval of a sermon.

Hiram was a retired man with a strong opinion on most matters. In the little country church he was appreciated because of his commitment to the congregation and especially because of his ability to play the organ. He was the only one in the church with that skill, so he normally was there playing competently for the hymns and special numbers.

But when Hiram didn't care for a sermon, he had no intention of sitting still for it. He didn't want to interrupt, objecting vocally to what the minister was saying. He didn't want to remain silent either, as part of a captive audience. So he had found a way to deal with the situation. He just got up, walked to the side door, and went home! It wasn't noticeable; he did it quietly. It became noticeable, however, when it was time for the final song!

The minister called me to vent his frustration. "I don't know what to do with him!" he exclaimed. "He has such strong opinions. I can't tailor make every sermon to his viewpoint! You'd think he could endure a new approach to a subject, maybe even let himself grow a bit. I don't think I can put up with this much longer!"

I let the minister talk, smiling inwardly. There wasn't much choice; Hiram was a life-long member of the church. He was never going to go away, and he was the only organist available.

I told my minister friend about the problems they were having in another congregation. There, the organist had a habit of sitting at the organ throughout the sermon, which in that church was very visible to everyone in the pews. Many Sundays that organist expressed the opinion that the sermon was boring. How? By laying her head down on the keyboard, going to sleep, and snoring! "I think they'd prefer that she leave!" I said.

The minister smiled, but offered the observation that pointing out a worse situation didn't solve his problem.

I had attended a seminar on preaching some years ago in which the speaker had said that there was a way to deal with controversial topics. "Before you preach, go to the person whom you know will be offended," he suggested. "Tell the person that you are going to preach on the subject and what you intend to say. Explain that it is a matter of conscience to you, and you feel you have no other choice. Then give him the option to argue with you in private, or even decide to be absent. He will respect you for it, and you'll keep a good relationship with the person. He'll appreciate the fact that you took him seriously enough to make the extra effort to tell him in advance."

My friend allowed that this was good advice, but that it wouldn't work in Hiram's case. "If he decides to be absent, what does that solve?" He had a point there.

I decided I'd talk with Hiram about it myself, with the minister's permission. Hiram explained that he did not want to be rude, and that he would resign as organist if required. However, he absolutely insisted that he would not remain for a sermon if he disagreed with the minister's views.

I said, "Hiram, you should be upset when you *do* agree with everything the minister says! That's when you should be upset, not when you disagree. If a minister makes you look at a subject in a different way, you may not agree, but he'll set you to thinking about it, and stretch your mind. It isn't threatening to just listen, think it over, and then maybe discuss it with the minister later in the week. You don't have to walk out!"

Hiram shook his head emphatically all the time I was talking. "Look, Doc," he said, "I like a good argument and I can give the other person the right to his opinion, but I'm danged if I'll sit still and listen to a lot of tripe when I never get a chance to talk back. What should I do? Shout out, 'I disagree?' Just sit there like a dummy? Silence implies consent! I just can't do it. I feel myself getting all hot and bothered inside; it sure as heck isn't a spiritual way to feel. I think the best thing I can do, before I explode, is just get out of there and cool off! They can sing one song without the organ, by golly!"

I had to report back to the minister that I'd tried, but failed, and I guessed he'd just have to live with the situation.

A few months went by, and then at a ministers' gathering Hiram's pastor came up to me with a big smile on his face. "Doc," he said, "I've solved the Hiram problem!"

I was amazed, but delighted. "How in the world did you do it?"

"I don't know why I didn't think of it before," he explained. We just rearranged our schedule. We used to have Sunday School at 9:45 and worship at 11:00. Now we have worship at 9:45 and Sunday School at 11:00."

"Fine," I replied, "but what did that solve?"

"Well, you see, we always had trouble getting a teacher for the adult class, but many of the adults brought their children to Sunday school. They'd just stand around talking, since most of them live too far away to go anywhere for an hour before church. As you know, in our little rural community there's no place else to go."

"Sure," I replied, "but so what?"

"I got the idea of having Sunday school after worship, and inviting all the adults to a session of 'Roast the Preacher.' I told them that whatever subject I preached about, we'd discuss it further after worship. So while the children are in Sunday School their parents, and others, meet with me and they can talk back, or ask questions, about what I had to say."

"Hiram loves it! He told me the other day, 'Preacher, the more controversial your sermons are, the better I like it! I can't wait for the Roast the Preacher time, and I can get you straightened out!"

"He never walks out anymore. I can see him occasionally turning a little red in the face. Then he grabs his little pocket notebook and writes a few notes. I know he's getting ready for me!"

"Actually, it frees me up a lot. I tell them my point of view about social issues, everything from gun control to abortion. For instance, I explain why I think Christians, as peacemakers, should support the outlawing of assault weapons. I used to worry if I was getting too political, now I don't because everybody has a chance to debate the subject later."

"You're a pretty creative guy," I replied. "I don't think this system would work everywhere, but if it works for your church and for Hiram, I'm delighted."

Hiram couldn't afford to walk out now. He had to hear all the points so he would know how to respond. And guess what? Now that he stays all the way through the sermon and hears all the arguments, he says sometimes he even gets convinced!

25

# 6

## *The Hugging Match*

"If those two are so determined to fight," I exclaimed to my wife, "I think we should just put them in a boxing ring at our next regional assembly, sell tickets, and make some money off it!" I was exasperated. Neither pastor would budge an inch, and their quarrel was going to wreck both congregations if they didn't get it settled. And they wouldn't accept any of my obviously wise suggestions!

I had been there countless times with innumerable suggestions and had used up all my intercessory skill. I was at my wit's end.

The problem was that both congregations shared the same building. The church, in Brooklyn, had originally been a predominantly white, English-speaking congregation. As the neighborhood changed it gradually became mainly black, with most of its members being Jamaican. An African American pastor was called and the Sunday service became more typical of black worship, by which I mean longer, more enthusiastic, and with more congregational participation. It wasn't so important to start on time, but everyone enjoyed the service and it was very important not to end too early! It was refreshing to me to meet with people who did not feel it was important to dismiss promptly at 12:00 noon.

There were still a few white members of the church,

including one prominent family. Mr. Pile's parents had been charter members, and his mother had played the organ until her death. Mr. Pile remained as Chairman of the Board, but he gave the black pastor his full support and did not seem to mind the change in style of worship.

Eventually the neighborhood changed again, this time by an influx of Hispanic people. One day a group of Hispanics asked if they could use the fellowship hall, which was the euphemism for the cellar, for worship. They did not have the funds to rent or buy a building of their own, and they would be grateful if they could use the downstairs facilities. The black congregation thought that was a good idea, which gave them a chance to help another congregation get started. Both groups belonged to the same denomination, but since the Hispanics worshiped in a different language it was considered necessary to worship separately.

Things went along in this way for awhile with no problems, as far as I knew. However, with the changes in neighborhood population continuing, it was not long until the new Hispanic congregation actually outnumbered the black worshipers upstairs. Finally the Hispanics numbered over 100 people on Sunday morning, and they were terribly cramped in the fellowship hall. Meanwhile the English-speaking congregation, which had declined to thirty or so persons, rattled around in a sanctuary meant to seat 300.

At this point the Hispanics asked if they could begin to use the sanctuary. They were willing to meet at a different hour on Sunday morning, but they wanted more space, a more beautiful setting, and access to the organ. The black congregation considered this and decided the request was reasonable, but not on Sunday morning at 11:00! That hour belonged to them! The Hispanics said they would be glad to meet at 9:30. So far, so good. Or so I thought.

Now Hispanics and Jamaicans may speak a different language, but one thing they have in common is joy in worship, and joy in *length* of worship! Like their African American brothers and sisters, our Hispanic congregation was in no hurry to have their worship end. Soon I began to hear complaints that their service was not over by 11:00 and the black folk were waiting in the narthex. Sometimes they waited until 11:30! Sometimes some of their members just gave up in disgust and went home.

The black pastor, Rev. Jamison, explained to the Hispanic minister, Rev. Rodriguez, that something had to be done. He reminded him of their agreement. But Rev. Rodriguez replied, "Friend, we can determine when a service begins but only God decides when it will end. What would you have me do if at 10:55 someone requests prayer, or comes forward with a testimony? Can I quench God's Spirit? No, Brother, God has blessed us with growth while your group has grown smaller. Now is the time for your congregation to begin to use the fellowship hall so there will be no conflict in times."

Rev. Jamison reported the conversation to his Board, and Mr. Pile was quickly on his feet. "This is outrageous," he thundered. This is like the camel that put his nose under the tent and then eased his way in until the Arab was pushed right outside! We helped these people and now they are turning their mother church out! Not only that, but the organ is upstairs, the organ my mother played all these blessed years, and I could not worship downstairs and never hear that organ again!"

So the issue was joined. My phone began to ring off the wall as both pastors urged me to intervene, on their side, of course! Knowing I was dealing with Christian folk, people of good will, I made a trip to Brooklyn for an especially-called meeting to solve the problem, confident that this would not be difficult to do.

In retrospect, I believe both congregations had said to their respective pastors, before my arrival, "Be strong! Don't betray us! Don't compromise!" At least both men seemed to enter the meeting with that attitude.

I asked them to propose solutions. Neither group saw anything good at all in what the other group had to say. Could the Hispanics meet earlier? No, some of them came from too great a distance. Could they meet later? No, because many had afternoon jobs. Could we have a bilingual service? That would prolong the service and would be annoying to both groups. Could the English-speaking congregation meet at another time? Never! Could they take turns? Should we draw straws? Could we bring in an outside mediator? Nothing, absolutely nothing, was acceptable.

After the first meeting failed, another was scheduled. And another. And another! All with the same results. In the meantime the irritation and resentment between the two groups continued to grow. The Hispanics pointed out that they had paid for most of the building maintenance and utilities for the last few years, and that the incorporation papers had been changed so that both congregations shared in the ownership of the property. The English-speaking people declared that had been their great mistake, for little did they realize their daughter church would turn them out and trample on their feelings.

I urged them to remember that we really were all one Church. "Surely we can compromise a bit," I pleaded. If the Hispanic group met even fifteen minutes earlier and the English group fifteen minutes later, would not that extra thirty minutes provide a buffer?" No way! It couldn't be done!

At this point I came up with the idea of the boxing match. Of course I knew it wasn't going to happen, but it seemed to be as constructive a suggestion as any other. Let the winner have the building and let his defeated opponent slink away, never to be seen again! What a way for church folk to solve a problem!

Rev. Higgins, an African American pastor who worked in the church's national office, called a few days later about another matter. I had always liked Roy Higgins. He was big and boisterous, but with a hearty laugh and twinkling eyes. He never let his position on the national staff go to his head, but seemed always eager to get the "business" over with so he could just ask how you were doing and maybe tell stories over a cup of coffee. Since he was on the phone I decided to ventilate and told him my frustration in trying to deal with these two recalcitrant pastors. "I'm just sick of both of them," I concluded.

Roy was silent for a moment, and then said, "Would you like for me to come talk to them?" I hadn't expected that offer, but I jumped at it.

"It couldn't do any harm, Roy," I said. "And if it does no good, at least it will be one more attempt to help. Besides that, it will get you into town and we can visit!" I'll admit the latter was a large part of my motive, since I held little hope for the meeting. What could he say or do I hadn't already tried?

A few weeks later I met Roy's plane and was glad to see him lumbering through the causeway door, a big grin on his face. "Hi, Doc!" he said, gripping my hand. I took his worn satchel in my other hand and began talking as we headed down the hall toward the exit from the airport and the parking lot.

"I'm glad you're here," I said, "but you can't believe what we're getting into! These two men are like bulls with locked horns. Neither will tolerate any suggestion and I think they don't even listen. They both just say, 'My way is the only way!' "

Roy didn't say much as we drove to the church, and he really didn't say much as the meeting progressed. It was a rehash of all the same old arguments. "Why don't you move downstairs? You were happy to have us meet there when we were small in number, and now it is your turn!"

"Well, why don't you act with some gratitude that you have a place to worship? Can't you meet other times rather than during our one hour?" And so it went.

Suddenly, without warning, Roy spoke up. "Jimmy," he said, addressing Rev. Jamison by his first name, "stand up!" He said it quietly, and it caught everybody by surprise. Rev. Jamison looked puzzled, but he laid his papers on the adjoining chair and got to his feet, looking at Roy questioningly. "Now you, Rafael," he said to Rev. Rodriguez. "You stand up too."

With a suspicious glance, Rev. Rodriguez complied.

The congregation, and I, sat in silence as the two ministers stood facing each other. We all wondered what was coming next. Then Roy asked, "How long has it been since you two hugged each other?"

After a long pause, Jimmy Jamison shook his head and grinned. "I don't reckon I have ever hugged him!" he said. Rev. Rodriguez slowly shook his head negatively also. "Nunca," he said. "Never."

Roy appeared to be thunder-struck. "What?" he exclaimed. "I can hardly believe it! You two have never hugged each other! Two brothers! Two ministers of the same church! Two men dedicated to the Gospel of love! Never hugged! Well, let's remedy that right now! Jimmy, go over there and give your brother a big hug!"

What could he do? Looking hesitantly at Rafael Rodriguez, Jimmy Jamison started across the room. As he neared him, Rev. Rodriguez suddenly smiled and the tension was broken. He reached out and the two embraced, patting each other on the back. Everyone in the room was smiling, with a few laughing out loud.

"Good!" Roy said. "Now you two hug more and argue less and we'll get our problems solved and get on with being a church! Let's go home now!"

I was surprised at the sudden dismissal of the meeting, but decided to trust Roy's intuition. "But Roy," I protested as we drove back to our hotel, "didn't we miss a prime moment? Wasn't that the moment right then to get this thing solved? Won't they just go home and then next Sunday the problem is still there?"

"Don't push it," Roy advised. "Let the Spirit have some working time!"

It was about two weeks later when my phone rang. It was Jimmy Jamison. "Doc," he said, "I've got some good news for you! Rafael and I have come to some conclusions we think our congregations will accept. He's willing to urge his folk to come at 9:00 and mine will wait until 11:15 to begin. To tell the truth, we hardly ever started on time anyhow, even before the Hispanic group came. And once a quarter we're going to have a union service in both languages."

I could hardly believe my ears. I couldn't help but remember that both of those suggestions had been rejected before, but I was happy to forget that. Was this problem really coming to an end?

"But Doc," Jimmy continued, "I feel real bad about you. I don't know why we didn't get this worked out all the times you came. I hope you don't feel hurt that we did it for Rev. Higgins."

"I don't feel badly, Jimmy," I assured him. "And you didn't do it because of Rev. Higgins; you did it because of a hug. I once thought you two men were so stubborn you should just settle this in a boxing match, but I've learned a hugging match is far better. In a hugging match everybody wins!"

# 7

## *I Am Unanimous in That*

When I was invited to attend the General Assembly of the Presbyterian Church, U.S.A. as an ecumenical advisory delegate I was excited and honored. It would be a great experience to go to the national meeting of this great church, participate in its deliberations, and meet many new people. As an advisory delegate I wasn't sure how much I would be involved, but I was ready to do my best.

The role that I was assigned to play was greater than I had anticipated. There were fifteen ecumenical advisory delegates and we were allowed to sit in the main hall with voting machines before us. Each delegate had a little machine on a table in front of him, or her, which looked a lot like a TV remote control. On this machine you could record a yes or no vote. Once the votes were tallied, a bar chart appeared on a large screen at the front of the hall showing the results of the vote.

We met in a large convention center. There were approximately 500 voting delegates plus many staff members, friends, and interested people. There were also youth advisory delegates, advisory delegates from other nations, and advisory delegates from theological schools.

We were taught how to use the machines. It was explained that once the light went on we had eight seconds to record our vote. We could change it, if we wished, during that time, but once the eight seconds had elapsed and the light gone out, the vote was final. The results appeared on the screen for all to see almost immediately.

There were many issues to be decided; everything from electing a moderator to voting on amendments to amendments. In each case, the presiding officer would say, "Advisory delegates, you may vote now." Then in a few seconds we would see how the ecumenical advisory delegates, the overseas advisors, the student advisors, and the youth advisors, felt on the issue.

After that, the screen would go blank and the moderator would intone, "Commissioners, you have been advised. You may vote now." Then the elected commissioners, whose vote really counted, would vote.

It was somewhat overwhelming to be one of fifteen advisory delegates and to know that all of the Presbyterian commissioners, who were truly members of the denomination and with a great stake in the outcome of votes, would be "advised" by what we thought! It caused me to read the papers into the night, speak with many people, and try to give good advice.

Usually the ecumenical delegates split their votes. We rarely voted unanimously. Often, however, we found ourselves 80 percent or more in agreement on major issues.

The Assembly lasted for many days. Presbyterians take it seriously and work hard! Some evenings it was after 10:30 before the work concluded.

On about the fifth day some of the ecumenical delegates had to leave. They apologized and left reluctantly, but due to their own positions and time constraints they had to go. That was a loss.

It was on the sixth evening, feeling very tired, that I began to think maybe I would leave the hall early and get some needed rest. With 7:00 a.m. breakfasts and these late evenings, I was tired. I thought maybe I could slip out at 9:30 p.m. or thereabouts and nobody would notice.

But the voting was still going on and being recorded for all to see. I noticed on the last vote that we ecumenical advisory delegates had all voted "Yes." That was unusual. Our votes were never unanimous.

The next issue to be decided was more controversial, but to my amazement the ecumenical delegates were also unanimous in their opinion on that too. "Well," I thought, "they all agreed with me on this. We're really getting our act together!"

The next two matters also found the ecumenical delegates unanimous. What was going on here?

Looking around, I discovered that all the ecumenical delegates except me had left! I was the only one voting; the whole assembly hall was getting to see what old Doc thought each time before they voted. I wondered how many people realized what was going on.

Some people seated near me did, and one lady began to giggle. Leaning over, she whispered, "Doc, enjoy it. You'll never have this much power in the church again."

I wasn't sure I wanted that much power.

I also realized that now there was no way I could leave. If I didn't stay and vote, the screen would be blank and everyone would realize that all the ecumenical delegates were absent. So I stuck with it for another hour, recording my one hundred percent votes on each issue dutifully.

I remembered one British comedy on television called "Are You Being Served," in which Mrs. Slocum, when she felt strongly on an issue, would insistently state her opinion and then add, "And I am unanimous in that!"

Doc, the ecumenical advisory delegate, was unanimous in all his opinions and advice that evening.

I hope I didn't do too much damage. They took my advice a lot, though! Maybe they would have voted that way anyhow.

But I agree I'll never have nor desire that much power again.

# 8

## *Caroling at the Hog Bar*

I've been caroling during the Advent season many times with many precious memories. Despite my off-key voice, I can join in the singing and at least at Christmas nobody cares how badly I sing! It's the Christmas spirit that counts.

When I think back over many caroling occasions, however, I always smile when I think about the time we went caroling at the Hog Bar.

The Hog Bar was an establishment of long standing in a small rural town known as East River not far from the local church which I served. People had gathered there for a few drinks and conversation after work for over a hundred years. Meals were served too, but the main function of the Hog Bar was just to serve as a gathering place in the evening.

The youth group from my church traditionally traveled out of the city to this small community for their caroling partly because their former youth counselors lived there and had taken them there in years past, but more importantly, they could go sing at the Hog Bar! The old codgers would turn on their bar stools, listen to the youthful voices raised in song, and then give them tips! What a highlight of the evening!

This year we had new counselors, Ben and Betty Green. They had joined our church recently coming from a much more conservative church. I worried about that, but we had nobody else willing to serve as counselors, and I reasoned that I always

36

attended the sessions too and could help balance their influence if they became too reactionary for the kids to handle. And, to give them credit, they were willing to attend faithfully and work hard. They had no problem with going to East River, but they didn't know about the Hog Bar yet.

So we set forth as usual, with a caravan of cars, for our caroling pilgrimage. When we arrived in East River we first went to the home of Mr. And Mrs. Trout. That was a tradition too. Mrs. Trout was blind, and she loved to have us come. Mr. Trout didn't love to have us come; he usually retreated upstairs and stayed out of sight for the duration of our visit. He didn't care for "the racket." But she would go to the piano, and as soon as she heard a familiar carol she would play the accompaniment by memory. We always enjoyed doing that, partly for the pleasure it gave her and partly to annoy her husband. After all, that's the way teen-agers, and some ministers, are!

As we went down the street we stopped at each house to sing. Some people invited us in for hot chocolate or cookies; others simply came to the door and beamed at us with pleasure. Still others didn't respond. Never mind; we sang lustily for them all.

As we continued on down the street I couldn't help but wonder whatever had happened to Penny. Penny was a young woman from East River who had started coming to the church I served some years ago. She was radiantly beautiful but deeply confused. She had married in haste at 18, divorced at 19, married again before the year was over, and then separated from husband number two. The last I knew, she was living with someone else. Penny had asked me if I would marry them, but I told her I wouldn't promise anything until we had some meetings for marriage counseling. She didn't accept that condition.

Despite the fact that she didn't want marriage counseling, Penny nevertheless was still my friend. I knew that she was searching for fulfillment in life, really searching for God. I wasn't going to give up on her. We had had many talks and I knew the good things about Penny. She just seemed to have poor judgment when it came to choosing men!

I wanted to help her, but I didn't think just performing a wedding would do that. Since then I hadn't seen her; I was afraid I had seen the last of Penny. I knew that she and her friend lived somewhere in East River, but I had no idea where. I thought it was pretty unlikely that we'd blunder onto them.

Soon we drew near the Hog Bar and the kids started getting excited. "Wow! There's the Hog Bar! Let's go sing for the drinkers!"

I was sorry that someone blurted that out! I had hoped to get into the Hog Bar before the Greens were forewarned. They were sure to object.

Our first conflict had been over a dance in the fellowship hall. The Greens had complained about it. I explained to them that the dance, like the caroling, was an annual tradition. It was well chaperoned, perhaps even better than the ones at the high school. "Think of it this way," I offered. "The sanctuary is for worship, the educational unit is for our Sunday School, and the fellowship hall is for recreation and fun. This dance is being held where it belongs."

The Greens assured me that they understood my point, but they felt dancing had no place in the church so they would not come, nor would their son. I had to find other sponsors for that one evening. But they hadn't resigned; that was hopeful.

I shouldn't have been surprised now, therefore, as they reacted in horror at the idea of our going into the Hog Bar. "Certainly not!" Ben had ordered. "We will not go in there."

I could see the disappointment on the young people's faces. They looked at me, and I knew we were going to have a crisis on our hands if I didn't find a way out of this stalemate.

"Now Ben, wait a minute. We are going here to witness! Where would it be better to go sing about the birth of Christ! We're not going to drink; we're going to tell sinners about the coming of a Savior. It's evangelism!"

That gave him pause. I could see I was on the right track.

"Think of the words of 'God Rest Ye Merry Gentlemen!' I continued. We even sing, 'And saved us all from Satan's power when we were gone astray!' "

Ben glanced at his wife, whose face was blank. "You really think it would be all right?" he asked.

"Absolutely!" I declared, and hurried forward with the kids before he had time to think about it.

We joyfully entered the Hog Bar and the youth let loose with "Joy to the World" with enthusiasm. Old men turned on their stools and smiled. Some were always there and expected this as much as our youth group did. Everyone seemed happy to see these red-cheeked youngsters full of youthful zest.

Suddenly I heard a female voice cry out, "Doc!" Turning, I saw Penny headed my way. She had been sitting at the end of the bar. She was beautiful as usual, in a form fitting red dress. "Merry Christmas, Doc!" she exclaimed, as she rushed to me and threw her arms around my neck.

"Merry Christmas, Penny," I responded, "and I hope the coming year will be a really good one for you." Somehow I couldn't even look at the Greens. How could I explain this? I didn't believe that Penny had even been in church since they came; they wouldn't know she was one of my flock.

Some things just can't be explained, and some things get worse the more you try to explain them. I'm glad Penny heard the carols and still felt at ease around me. After all, it was Christmas!

# 9

## *Getting Ready to Live*

When Mrs. Trout phoned me and began the conversation by saying, "Doc, get down here! I think I'm going to die!", I was truly alarmed.

"What has happened?" I asked. "Are you hurt?"

"No, no," she said, "I'm just old, and I have some serious health problems. I don't need to go into all that. But the doctor tells me that I may not have much longer to live, and I feel in my bones that is true. Now, I need you to get me ready to die!"

That is quite a summons, but I thought I'd better respond. So that very afternoon I drove down to East River to visit with Mrs. Trout.

"Doc," she said, "how do we know there is any life after this one anyway?"

"Mrs. Trout," I responded, "you are a Christian; you know the Bible message. And here we are at Easter time, even as we speak. Jesus rose from the dead, and we have the gift of life eternal."

She regarded me skeptically. "Doc," she said, "I have read Matthew, Mark, Luke, and John. I find those resurrection stories quite inconsistent and hardly convincing!"

There is a great problem in reconciling the events of the resurrection stories into a consistent time period, as Bible scholars know. That doesn't stop us from getting the point of the stories; that life is stronger than death and love overcomes hate and life with God can be eternal. Yet somehow this didn't seem to be the right time to launch into all of that with Mrs. Trout. So I tried another tack.

"Mrs. Trout," I offered, "then think of this. God is Love. God so loved the world that he sent Christ. The whole message of the Gospel is that God loves us. Now, why should the wearing out of a physical body put an end to something spiritual like God's love? Can't God take care of you and love you even when your body doesn't work any more?"

She thought about that. "I have known love all my life," she said. "I think maybe I can hold onto that."

When I left the house I was worried about her. I loved Mrs. Trout. She was one of those few people who could say exactly what she thought, even to a minister, and not worry about it. She was not intimidated, and she was not deceitful. With Mrs. Trout you got what you saw and saw what you got.

Despite her blindness she was the best informed member of the congregation. I had had many a talk with her about world events and current issues. By the means of tapes and records and books in Braille she stayed on top of things. And she didn't deal in platitudes! I smiled when I thought of her saying the resurrection stories were inconsistent and not convincing.

I thought I would call on her again soon to see if she was improving. If she truly was dying, I'd have to talk and pray with her a lot more.

So it was with amusement and relief when, about a week later, she phoned me again. "Doc, " she exclaimed, "the doctor says I'm doing better than he expected. You got me all ready to die and now it looks like I'm not dying! So get back down here and help me get ready to live!"

With pleasure!

# 10

## *The Bodyguard*

I don't ride a bus often anymore, but on this occasion there was no other way to get to my destination. In New York City I ride the subway. But in this remote section of Missouri, since I didn't have a car, the bus was the only possibility for my travel.

A program of education in conflict intervention was being offered at a retreat center. I had been told to take the bus from the airport to a nearby town, and then to phone the retreat center. A car would come pick me up.

As I waited in the bus station for the departure time, I noticed an interesting appearing man. He was about five feet eight inches tall, and looked to me like a cowboy. Although he was not a large man, and quite slim, he was very muscular. Once I saw him stretch by leaning over backward farther than I could comfortably do! He wore jeans, a baggy leather jacket, and cowboy boots. I wondered who he was.

When we got onto the bus, I was pleased when he sat down beside me. Somehow I knew he was going to be an interesting character. I started a conversation.

"Well, we have a long ride in the night," I said. "I'm on my way to a retreat center. How about you?"

"I'm going on to Kansas City," he said. "I have work there."

"What do you do?"

"I'm in security."

"Oh," I said. "I understand. You are a guard at a factory, or something like that?"

"No, not that kind of security," he said. "I don't guard places, I guard people. There is a man who has had some threats so I am going to protect him."

This was interesting. I'd never met a bodyguard before!

I remembered that he had said he was going all the way to Kansas City. "Why are you taking the bus?" I asked. "You could have flown there."

"X-ray machines!" he responded. "I can't go through them, carrying weapons."

"Oh!"

"I only guard good guys," he assured me. "I don't guard crooks."

"I'm glad."

"If you ever need protection, I'm your man."

I said I'd remember that.

Now it was his turn to ask questions. "What do you do?"

I explained that I was a regional minister. He didn't pick up on the "regional" part of that, but was very interested that I was a "preacher." He immediately launched into a series of questions, and I began to feel that the answers I gave were not what he wanted to hear.

"So you're a preacher, huh? What do you think about these women preachers?"

"Some of them are really great," I said. "In Christ there is neither male nor female, and we're getting more women ministers all the time. They are doing a great job."

"Harummmmph!" That was the only response I got to that.

I threw the question back at him, to see whether or not we were in agreement. "What do you think about women preachers?" I asked. He totally ignored my question, but continued his own grilling of me.

**43**

"How about abortion? What does your church teach about that?"

I tried to explain briefly that we have "no creed but Christ," and that Christians were free to disagree on such an issue. I continued, "I myself am pro choice but anti abortion. In most cases I think abortion is wrong, or a tragedy, but there are circumstances in which it is the least bad choice available. I don't think we need for the legislatures to decide; I think the woman must seek to know God's will in her situation and then make her own decision."

That brought a louder "Harrummmmmph!" than the first answer.

I wondered what kind of arms the bodyguard was carrying! I also wondered how much longer it would be before I could get off the bus! I wished I had already had my training in conflict management! What next?

"What about those homosexuals?" God *help* me!

I tried to stay brave, but I was faltering. "What do you think?"

"What do you think?" He was asking the questions.

"Well, as in the case of abortion, in my church each person can have his own opinion. You can have your opinion. I think it is more genetic than chosen; I think you can't be prejudiced against people for being who they are from birth. I think we should try to be brothers and sisters to everyone, and not try to be their judges."

"Harrummmmmmph!! Harrummmmmmph!!"

Where is that retreat center?

"How about other religions? Do you know anything about the Indians' religion?"

"Not much," I said. "I wish I knew more. I think we have a lot to learn from them. I believe in taking care of the environment and living in harmony with nature; they do that. I heard a story once about an Indian chief who told a missionary, 'We always knew about this God; we just didn't know his name.' "

I'd finally given a good answer. The bodyguard told me that he had had much contact with Native Americans, and in fact, said he had been adopted into one of the tribes. He began to recount their beliefs for me and why they knew more about the Great Spirit than the churches did. I was glad he was talking about it and not asking any more questions. I also was interested in what he had to say.

Suddenly the bus slowed. The driver said, "This is the stop for the retreat center." It was time for me to go.

"Goodbye," I told him, "and good luck with your protecting good people!" He nodded goodbye.

As the bus drove away, I remembered that I had never gotten his name. He had offered to protect me if I ever needed help, but I had no idea how to contact him. It may be just as well. He said he protected only good guys, and I'm not sure he found me qualified!

# 11

## *The Kiln*

When you live on the border of another country, contact is frequent!  Since my home is one block from the Niagara River and Canada is right across a nearby bridge, it is not anything unusual to cross over for a meal, shopping, or to visit friends.  But a few years ago the crossings became much more numerous because of the lower price of gasoline in Canada.

When you can save 30 cents per gallon, it is well worth the time and the $1.00 toll to take 30 extra minutes and go fill up there!

The lower prices in Canada no longer prevail, but a few years ago when they did, I made it a habit to buy my gasoline there.  So one Sunday morning, as Betty and I were heading for the Niagara Falls church, I decided to be a half-hour late for Sunday School and go buy gas.  "Betty," I said, "I'll drop you off at the church and you can tell people I'll be there in a few minutes.  I'm not teaching anyway, and I want to fill up the tank."

Betty gave me one of those looks that says, "What a poor decision," but nevertheless I did as I said and drove the extra few blocks to the border crossing.

The inspector at the border asked, as he always does, "Where were you born?  What is the purpose of your visit?  How long will you be in Canada?  Are you importing anything you must declare?"

I gave the routine answers, but this time, after assuring him that I had nothing to declare, he asked, "What is that I see in your back seat?"

I looked behind me. I had forgotten all about it! There in its box was a new ceramic kiln which had been donated for our church camp. I had picked it up the day before, taken it home, and planned to deliver it to the camp on Monday.

"Oh, I forgot about that," I explained. "That's a new ceramic kiln that I'm taking to a church camp tomorrow."

"I'm sorry, Sir," he said, "but you can't take that into Canada without paying a duty on it."

"But I'm just going to that gas station over there!" I explained. "You can see it; then I'm coming right back. Let me just set it here on the ground and I'll pick it up when I return in five minutes!"

"We can't do that," he said. Then, sighing, he continued, "Bring it into our office."

I followed him in, wondering what was next. I had to fill out a form concerning the kiln and its worth and that I was leaving it. Then he told me that when I returned I'd have to come back in and fill out another form to retrieve it.

So I obliged, knowing that Betty would be able to note that it had taken me a good deal longer to go for gas than I had indicated.

I bought the gas, reclaimed my kiln, and hurried off to church.

That night I remembered that on Monday I needed to drive our van to work since I had to pick up several people to take to a meeting at the church camp with me. So I removed the kiln from the car and put it in the van so I wouldn't forget it the next day.

Monday morning I arose bright and early and started off for the church camp. I was excited; it always seemed like a day off when I went to the camp rather than to the office.

Humming to myself, I was breezing along when I happened to notice that I was low on gasoline. "Oh brother," I thought. But I can save so much money if I take a few minutes to cross over to Canada and fill up before going to the camp." So, veering from my normal path, I detoured about a half mile off to the east to go across the bridge to Canada.

Of course I met the same set of questions as before, and gave the same answers. However, the inspector was a different person from the one I had met yesterday. When he said, "What is that I see in the back seat?" I turned to look. Of course, there was the kiln again!

"Oh, gee, I totally forgot that!" I said. "That's a kiln that I'm taking to church camp."

"You can't take it into Canada, I'm afraid, without paying a duty on it, Sir."

"I know, I know, I'll just leave it with you while I get gas and then pick it up on my way back to the States."

"That isn't allowed, Sir," was his surprising response.

"Why not?" I asked. "The man who was here yesterday let me do it!"

The inspector regarded me in silence for a few moments with a bewildered expression on his face. Finally he said, "You bring this thing into Canada every day?"

"No, no," I said, "but I did bring it yesterday!"

He turned on his heel without a word and went into his office. He was gone for awhile; when he returned he had a book in his hand. He began to read: "Mr. Lamb, ceramic kiln. That must be you."

"Yes it is!" I exclaimed. "See, I did leave it yesterday!"

There was another long pause. Finally he said, "We aren't supposed to do this. In the interests of consistency, however, bring it in."

I did, filled out the form, left my kiln, and hastened away. This was getting ridiculous. Shame-facedly, I retrieved the kiln and thanked him, then hurried away.

As I left the inspector called after me: "Mr. Lamb?"
"Yes?"
"Do me a favor. Don't bring this damn thing back

**48**

tomorrow!"

This was not my only embarrassing border crossing. A worse experience happened one year just before I left for our Regional Assembly. I had the van full of sealed boxes with papers I needed to transport to the site of the Assembly. I had already loaded them all into the van before I realized I needed gas for the trip, so I hoped the inspectors would let me take them in. "After all," I reasoned, "they are of no value except to our people at the meeting. They're just a lot of paper."

I had 200 copies of financial reports, budgets, resolutions, reports, orders of worship, and song sheets. My secretary had carefully packed them and taped the boxes so they would not spill if I took any corners too fast.

I explained to the inspector, a young woman this time, what they were. However, since they were sealed, she seemed a bit suspicious. "Are they religious articles?" she asked.

Now, that question gave me pause! I guess budgets and financial reports can be religious articles. Or are they? Anyway, I decided the right answer was "Yes."

"Okay," she said. "I'll tell you what. Let's open just one box and if it is a religious article I won't bother opening the others."

That seemed fair. She picked one box at random, slit it open, and there on top were some resolutions with an interesting title. They read, "Resolution In Support of Illegal Aliens."

To my amazement, that didn't seem to bother her and she let me go on my way!

Our Haitian pastor, Matthew, was asked once if there were illegal aliens in his congregation. He answered, "Well, you and I both know that in the eyes of God, nobody is illegal. We are all God's children."

Someday we'll all be "crossing the border," and I think God won't ask us where we were born or how long we'll stay, or the purpose of our visit." God might ask us if we have anything to declare. Then we can answer, "We declare our love for You and your Son and all your people." Then I believe we'll be

**49**

welcomed, even without filling out any forms, with open arms!

# 12

## *Heaven's Ceiling Won't Fall*

After thirty years, I was on my way back to Kansas! I was really excited. Thirty years ago I had been a seminary student, serving a small rural parish. That had been a wonderful time. Now, after all these years, the pastor and board of that church had invited me to come conduct a week of preaching there. I couldn't wait.

I thought about the people in the church, and I knew that many of the ones I had known were still there. This church was composed mostly of farm folk who lived on the family homesteads generation after generation. Except for those who had passed on, they would still be there and remember me.

That thought suddenly gave me a moment of panic. Yes, they would remember me, and they all knew I was coming so there would be no doubt about who I was. On the other hand, I would be seeing people I had not seen for thirty years, and I probably would not remember all their names! I hoped I wouldn't hurt too many feelings.

I determined to say to them right away, "Look, if you had seen me walking down the street without knowing I was in town, you wouldn't have known me either!" Whenever we met someone, I would also ask the minister to tell me the person's name before I had to ask.

It was so kind of him to invite me back! Each year the church had a week of preaching, and he must have known how glad I would be to return to my place of pleasant memories.

**51**

I thought about my first summer there. One of the men in the church had come to see me as summer began to ask what my plans were. I explained that I would have to get a full-time job to earn the money to return to seminary in the fall. The church paid only for weekend services, but did provide a parsonage. I lived there, commuted to school four days a week, and served the church on the weekend and some evenings.

He told me the church wanted me to stay around all summer, and he wondered if I could do farm work. I assured him that I could learn! I had spent previous summers working with a construction crew, so I thought I could handle farm work. I'd have to learn how though!

He explained that he'd teach me. My job would be picking up hay bales, stacking them on a truck or sled, going to the barn, and then hoisting them up to the hay loft.

"Great," I replied. "When do I start?"

He stroked his chin for a few moments, thoughtfully. Finally he said, "You're soft; you've been in school so you aren't toughened up. We could use you Saturday, but we ought to take it easy on you the first few days. Don't come early; come at six!"

I found out he wasn't kidding; they usually started at dawn. The work was hard but good for me, both physically and also because of the contacts it gave me with the men of my congregation. I learned to respect them, and I became much more closely acquainted with them than ever could have occurred during visits in their living rooms.

The farmers passed me around all summer and kept me employed. I chuckled as I remembered that summer and the different farmers for whom I worked.

Each one had a different style of stacking the hay bales so they overlapped and tied together on the truck and would not slip. I would learn one farmer's way, only to be told by the next farmer that that was no way to stack hay! Then I'd have to learn his system.

One farmer's field was somewhat swampy, and to my

horror I found a black widow spider on a hay bale I had just handled. He calmed me down by asking me on what side of the hay bale I had seen it, top or bottom. "The bottom," I answered, puzzled. "What difference does that make?"

"Well, which side of the hay bale did you pull up against your chest when you lifted it?"

"The top," I had to admit.

"Of course," he said. "The spiders are between the hay and the ground, and that is the side of the hay bale away from you when you lift them. If one bites you, though, we'll take you straight to the hospital. You may get sick but people usually don't die."

Somehow I found that less than reassuring, and woke up that night from a bad dream, wildly brushing imaginary spiders off the bed.

Then there was Mr. Biggs. Mr. Biggs was not a farmer; he ran the local bar. I use the word "bar" loosely, in that the only alcoholic beverage it provided in legally dry Kansas was beer. Mr. Biggs' bar was really the town recreation hall. Men would come there, visit, play cards, and have a beer.

Mrs. Biggs was a member of my congregation, but her husband never attended. One day I decided that I should pay a visit on Mr. Biggs, so I walked up to the bar and over to the bar-stools to take a seat and talk with him.

"Well, hello, Doc," he said. "I'm sure you don't want a beer. What can I get you?"

"Just give me some conversation," I replied. "Mr. Biggs, your wife is always at our church services. I wish you could come with her some Sunday."

He threw his head back and laughed. "That will be the day!" he replied. "The ceiling will fall on me if I come in that door!"

I smiled, but shook my head negatively. "No it won't," I said. "We'll all be glad to see you, and I think you'll like it."

He grew serious. "You may be glad to see me," he answered, "but the others won't. They don't want me there."

I was indignant. "Of course they do!" I said. "You are invited, and welcome."

He thanked me, but continued to decline. I left feeling discouraged that he sincerely believed he would not be welcome in the congregation.

A few days later I began to wonder if he was right! One of our leading deacons dropped by the parsonage to see me. "I hear you've been up in the bar, Doc," he exclaimed.

"Yes I have," I answered, "but not drinking. I went there to see Mr. Biggs and invite him to church."

The deacon did not smile. Giving me a steely look, he leaned forward and peered directly into my eyes. "No Christian," he intoned, "goes in that place!"

"Wait a minute!" I said. "Jesus went not only to the homes of the tax collectors, but he also visited with prostitutes. I can go talk to anyone!"

"Then talk to him outside that bar, is my advice," he said.

In the time that followed I made a couple more visits to see Mr. Biggs, but without success. He was always cordial and glad to see me, but he was sure he wouldn't be welcome at the church unless he gave up the bar business.

Now, after all these years, I wondered if he was still alive and still in the bar! When my plane landed at the Wichita airport, I was met by the current pastor, who had invited me to come. As we drove back toward the little town where the church was located, I had lots of questions about the people I remembered. I also asked about Mr. Biggs.

He threw his head back and laughed. "You know, the other day I mentioned to the chairman of our Board that I had been up to see Mr. Biggs," he said. "The chairman said, 'Oh my gosh, I think you are the first minister to go see Mr. Biggs since Doc was here!' "

"Let's go see him again!" I said. The minister agreed.

So on about the third day of my visit the pastor and I made our way up to the bar, which looked exactly as it had thirty years ago. It looked the same inside too, except only a couple of older men were present. Younger people now went to the new video arcade! Of course Mr. Biggs was there, looking a lot older than I remembered. Of course he would after thirty years! He must have been about fifty when I was there as pastor, so that would make him eighty now.

To my pleasure, he remembered me. "Mr. Biggs," I said, "thirty years ago I asked you to come to church and you said the ceiling would fall in if you came. Now here I am, come all the way from New York to ask you again! I assure you the ceiling won't fall on you, and I want you to come!"

He laughed, but shook his head "no." I could tell he was pleased, though. "Doc," he said, "I've gotten along without the church and it's gotten along without me all these years. I guess we'll just leave it that way. I do believe in God; he knows it."

"It is good to make commitment, though, and be baptized," I said. "Wouldn't you like to take that kind of stand, and really be a member, and isn't it about time?"

"Thanks, Doc, but no thanks," he said. "I'm content."

We visited a bit, and then decided it was time to leave before the descendants of the deacon discovered that I was in the bar again. As I started out the door, Mr. Biggs called after me: "Doc, you seem to call on me every thirty years or so. Try me again thirty years from now, and maybe I'll come!"

Thirty years from now both Mr. Biggs and I may well be on the other side of the Pearly Gates. I'll bet he discovers that the ceiling of Heaven doesn't fall when he gets there!

# 13

## The Camping Trip

We were going camping for vacation, and I was excited! I love camping, but it is a wonder that I do. My first camping trip was a disaster.

Today going camping is pure joy. We get away, usually in the woods, with no possibility of the phones ringing. We make campfires and watch them hypnotically; I feel I have accomplished something wonderful if I can get the wood to burn up entirely before going to bed. To feel the wind blowing through the net sides of the little pop-up camper as I lie in bed and look up at the stars is paradise. But sometimes I remember that first camping trip and shake my head at my own stupidity.

We were so happy when we bought our first camper. It folded down when you were pulling it, but when you stopped and put it up it became quite large. I'm no mechanic, and it took me a while to get the hang of it, but I finally mastered it. Other people probably thought it was simple.

It had a table, which folded down to make a bed, plus beds on each end. It also had a tiny room so small that I could barely squeeze into it where a toilet was housed. Since we had a small baby at the time we bought it, it seemed important to have electricity, water hook ups, and a toilet indoors!

On our very first time out with the trailer we went to a beautiful wooded park. It took me quite a while to get the trailer leveled; there were jacks under each corner which needed to be raised or lowered to make the trailer secure so it wouldn't rock to and fro when you walked inside it. I got the electricity hooked up and then discovered there was no water connection. A neighborly fellow camper explained that I could carry water from a short distance away; that was no problem.

Our trailer came equipped with a sewer hose, which could be attached, underneath the trailer, to the toilet. Then by pulling a lever the waste from the toilet would go through the hose into the sewer outlet. But there was no sewer outlet at our camping spot either.

"Oh well," I told my wife, "they say the toilet has a holding tank and it doesn't have to be emptied every day."

The campground had a place to empty toilets near the entrance to the campground, but going there would require taking down the trailer. I had had so much trouble getting it up and leveled that I didn't want to do that.

After a few days of camping, we began to notice that our camper was developing a decidedly unpleasant smell. "That toilet," my wife informed me, "stinks! You need to do something about emptying it."

That was obviously true, but how?

Suddenly the answer became obvious to me. I may not be mechanically minded, but in this case I had the answer.

"Why not," I thought, "attach the sewer hose to the toilet, but carefully plug the other end of the hose? Then I can empty the holding tank and toilet into the hose, unattach it, and carry it to a nearby rest room?" Spaced throughout the campground there were restrooms with showers and toilets. "Then I can lower one end of the hose, empty it into a toilet, and flush!"

I waited until it was quite dark, since I didn't really want anyone to see what I was doing, but I saw no harm in it.

So, under cover of darkness, I went outside the trailer and attached the sewer hose. I used some old rags to stuff the far end of the hose. Then I pulled the lever and felt the hose move in my hands as it filled with waste from the toilet. When

I could tell that the toilet and holding tank were all empty, I took the hose off and lifted it up, holding each end of the hose up high with my hands.

Now I discovered unanticipated problems! My idea worked, but there were two things I had not realized. First of all, the hose stretched! I had to raise both hands as high as I could raise them, well over my head, to keep the center of the hose from touching the ground. The hose made a huge U, far longer than it appeared when it was empty and compact.

The second problem was that it was *heavy!* I had no idea that it would weigh so much.

Stretching to the utmost, and using all my strength, I staggered off in the dark toward the rest room. But where was it? For the life of me, I could not seem to find it! I walked up one street and back the next. My arms were killing me. "I simply must put this down," I would think, only to remember, "but if I do, it will empty! They would have to vacate this entire park, I think, if I let this hose empty!" So I would stagger on.

I made my way back to our camper and hissed, "Come out with a flashlight and help me!"

"I can't come now," she answered. "I'm busy with the baby."

"You'd *better* come now," I shouted, "or you and this whole trailer park will regret it!"

From the darkness I heard the voice of our friendly neighbor in the next camping spot. He couldn't see me through the trees, but he had heard me. "Can I help you?"

"NO!" I shouted. "Do not come over!" I'm sure I sounded quite unfriendly.

My wife peered out the door and seeing my predicament, broke into peals of laughter.

"It isn't funny!" I said. "This thing is going down any second now!"

She hurried out of the trailer with a flashlight, and guided me to the rest room, squealing with laughter all the way. "Please be quiet," I hissed, "or people will come to see what is so funny."

I made it to the rest room. I guess I had no choice. When I lowered one end of the hose into the toilet, it emptied as planned. Disaster averted.

My arms were sore for a week.

Later I learned that there are buckets, with lids, made for just this purpose. Campers empty their toilets regularly into the enclosed buckets and carry them for dumping in approved areas. How was I supposed to know that?

But you know what? As the years went by, the fear and irritation of the first camping trip have become a cause for hilarity in our family. Somebody once said, "Tragedy becomes humor ten years later." In our case, that is true.

So I still love camping. And as I lie in our camper, thinking back on our first trip, it just makes the present vacation a little more delightful. I can laugh at what happened in the assurance it will never happen to me again.

## 14

### *The Barn*

Rev. Peterson knew that Bernie and I had been friends for years, so he appealed to me to try to use my influence on him. "Doc," he sputtered, "Bernie is a fine man and he attends my church every Sunday, but he can't hold an office because he isn't a member. And I can't get him to join! He keeps saying he is a member of his home church in Oklahoma, and I can't get him to budge. Could you talk to him for me?"

I agreed readily. I had always enjoyed being with Bernie, and this gave me a great excuse to take a day off and drive out to the farm where he lived with his wife and some adult children.

As I drove to the farm, I thought about another occasion when a regular church attender had been reluctant to join the congregation. The minister had asked me for help then too.

He had phoned and explained that a lady had moved to his village from Georgia and had started attending regularly. So he called on her in her home and asked her to put her membership in the congregation.

"I am already a member," she informed him.

"I know you are already a member of a church," he replied, "but now that you live here, I thought possibly you would consider placing your membership with us. You can do it by transfer."

"No, I am already a member of your congregation," was

her response.

"How can you say that?" he asked. "You are attending, but you haven't joined!"

"When I joined THE CHURCH, she explained, I became a member of the Body of Christ wherever I am. So when I moved here, of course I came to worship with my people. We are members of each other because we are all in Christ."

That was pretty good theology, but it didn't fit the constitution!

"I understand," the minister told her, "and of course that's right. I wish everyone understood that when you move from one place to another, you should join the church where you now live. So why don't you come forward Sunday morning when we sing our final hymn, and I'll welcome you into the congregation?"

"No," she said. "You don't understand. I can't "join" your church! I am *already* part of it! To come forward would indicate I was joining something of which I'm already a member!"

"But," he sputtered, "according to our constitution, new members come by baptism or by transfer of membership. We need a letter from your former church or your statement of desire to reaffirm your commitment with us to add you to the rolls."

"I can't do that," she insisted. "I won't do anything to indicate I am out and coming in when I am already in!"

"So," the minister asked me, "what should I do? I want her to be a member, but she won't do anything to become one!"

I had laughingly responded, "I think you just got a new church member! Why don't you just announce next Sunday that your congregation is so pleased that she is now a member of your church? I wish we had more people who took it that seriously!"

But now I was on my way to see Bernie, who did *not* want to join the church, despite the fact that he was indeed a

**61**

part of it in every way except officially so. It wouldn't have made any difference except that he couldn't hold any office without membership. Sometimes our constitutions get in the way!

My nephew, who is Catholic, attends a Protestant church in Alaska and was asked to be treasurer. I asked the minister how they could do that when he was still a Catholic. He said, "Well, he comes, and he's good, and in Alaska we get a little informal about these things." Maybe he's right. Who knows?

With all these thoughts going through my mind, I pulled into the long driveway leading up to Bernie's farmhouse. I found him out in the back yard, raking up some left over leaves from last fall. We were glad to see each other; he invited me onto the back porch for some ice tea. After small talk, I got onto the subject of church membership.

"Bernie," I said, "you go to Fairview Church every Sunday. I know you are one of the regular people, and I know how much you love the Lord. Why don't you put your membership there?"

"Doc," Bernie said, "I'll bet my preacher's put you up to this. I told him and I'll tell you, my membership is in my HOME CHURCH back in Oklahoma. I was born there, baptized there, worshipped there, until I moved here. My parents were members of it until they died. It will always be my home church and I have a loyalty to it."

"I know, Bernie, and that's great, but you can still love it and love your church here. They could use you as a deacon or trustee. Why not put your membership here, but still keep in touch with your home church too?"

"I don't really keep in touch," Bernie confided. "I haven't been back there for years and years. But it is in my memory and my heart. I'll do whatever they ask me to do to help out here, but my membership stays in my home church in Oklahoma."

Just then Bernie's son Mark, who worked on the farm

with Bernie and lived in a smaller house they had built on a corner of the farm when Mark married, walked up and joined us. "Forget it, Doc," he advised. "We've all had this conversation with Dad many times. He won't budge."

I told Bernie the story of the lady who said she was already a member, because her membership went with her wherever she went. He wasn't moved. "That's fine for her," he said, "but I feel differently about it. My membership stays in my home church."

I dropped the subject before he became irritated. You can only push so much! And I reported back to Rev. Peterson that it was a no-go.

So it was with some surprise that I learned, about a year later, that Bernie had joined the church! I phoned to congratulate him and ask why, but got no answer. So I phoned his son Mark.

Mark was laughing. "Doc, I think I made the difference for him to join," he explained. I made a vacation trip back to Oklahoma to see relatives I hadn't seen for years. While I was there I decided to drive by the old "home church" for Dad's sake. To my amazement, it was stuffed to the roof with hay! It had been sold and a farmer was using it for storage. The congregation had closed several years ago; there were too few people to keep going. So when I got home I told Dad, 'Dad, guess what! You don't belong to any church at all anymore! You belong to a barn!'"

"The next Sunday he joined the church," Mark continued, chuckling. Rev. Peterson was glad and so was Momma. She'd been waiting for him to join her there for years. They've already made Dad a member of the evangelism committee. He says he wants to make sure the church grows and never closes like his home church did!"

I'm glad Bernie is a church member now, and not a barn member. It's better this way!

# 15

## *Breaking the Bread*

Churches in my denomination take Communion every Sunday. The sixty churches in my region do it sixty different ways. I never realized, until I started working in regional ministry, how many possible variations there could be to one service!

The minister may stand behind the Communion Table and offer words of institution; then the elders pray. Perhaps one elder prays for the bread and then it is distributed to the people. The second elder then prays and the cup is distributed. Or, maybe one elder prays for both and both are taken into the congregation simultaneously. Sometimes people eat the bread when it is brought to them; sometimes they hold it and all eat together. Same with the cup. Or maybe they eat the bread individually and take the cup in unison.

Maybe they come forward. In one church, the minister is handed a bowl and washes his hands before breaking the bread. Some churches use a real loaf of bread; others use little individual cubes of bread that are already separated.

You get the idea. I could go on and on about the different ways Communion is observed in churches of the same denomination!

Of course each church thinks the way it does it is the normal way. I go from church to church, but most people attend the same one each Sunday. So their tradition, observed week after week seems normative to them. To me, each Sunday is a surprise.

Even after I visit a church and participate in Communion, it may be a year or more before I return there. I can't keep all the varieties of practice in mind.

A hazard of my job is that many times I am asked to preside at the Communion Table. This is an honor; it is also a problem. After years of serving as Regional Minister I'm sure many people think, "He still can't get it right! He always seems hesitant, looking at the pastor for clues. Why can't he learn how it is done?"

One Sunday I was to be the preacher at one of our larger congregations. First Church's sanctuary was built as a vaulted cathedral; everything lent itself to formal worship. The pulpit was high, up several steps, and the Communion Table was on a raised platform in the chancel area. Usually I arrive at a church early, but this particular Sunday I made it barely in time for the service to begin. Therefore I had no time to ask questions.

The presiding elder whispered to me as we walked down the aisle during the processional, "All you need to do today is preach and preside at Communion. We'll take care of the Scripture, offering, and everything else."

I was prepared for the sermon, but I realized at once I was not familiar with this church's particular ritual for Communion. However, I could see a loaf of bread and a pitcher and chalice of wine on top of the Communion Table. "This is obviously one of the churches that uses real bread and performs the symbolic act of literally breaking the bread," I thought. I knew what to do.

After the sermon, it was time for the sacred moment of Holy Communion. This is the time when the Gospel is proclaimed even if the minister has failed to do so during the sermon. In the breaking of bread and pouring of wine, the death of Christ for our sins is remembered and effective. I like the actual breaking of a loaf as part of the service.

**65**

I proceeded to the Communion Table and raised the loaf in my hands. All the eyes of the people were on me, more intensely than usual, I thought. "On the night when he was betrayed our Lord took bread," I intoned, "and he blessed it and broke it..." As I said these words I gripped the bread and pulled downward, but nothing happened. The bread felt very tough. Not wanting to delay or ruin the beauty of the moment, I exerted more pressure.

Suddenly there was a loud POP and the loaf broke, with pieces flying left and right. I suddenly realized that what I was holding was a decorative, shellacked loaf! I was horrified. One of the elders, belatedly, reacted, telling me, "Reverend, the Communion bread is on trays under the top of the table." I discovered a little ledge under the table-top on which the plates were waiting.

"I'm sorry. Forgive me," I murmured, picking up the trays and handing them to the elder. He managed to pray, although I noticed he stopped often and his lips seemed to be twitching. After I opened my eyes, I saw that half the congregation was quietly laughing, hiding their mouths behind their hands or wiping their eyes with the handkerchiefs. They were not angry or horrified; just terribly amused.

After church, of course, people had something to say to me at the door other than "Nice sermon." "We'll never forget the Communion service!" One would say. "You have a real talent for breaking bread, Reverend!" "Are you going to pay for the loaf you broke, or fix it?"

It was two years later before I went back to First Church. I was glad they were trusting me to lead their worship again. This time I arrived early, in plenty of time for instructions and review of procedures. I noticed that there was a new shellacked loaf on the Communion Table, just like the one I had broken previously.

Before church at least four people said to me, "You aren't going to break the loaf again today, are you Doc?" I assured them I would not.

I met with the choir for a few words and prayer, and then we began the processional. As we approached the front of the church I noticed that the decorative loaf was missing! I had seen it there a half hour earlier, but someone had removed it before I entered the sanctuary. I guess they were taking no chances!

# 16

## *The Ministerial War*

Allen and Alex hated each other!  Since I loved them both, that was a problem, not only to them, but to me.

It had started when one of Allen's key church families grew dissatisfied with their church.  The dissatisfaction centered on the lack of Bible study.  They were serious about it, and wanted to plunge into the Scriptures in a systematic way.

The Herrons talked with their pastor about it.  He told them he planned to start a Bible study group on a weeknight soon, but as weeks went by it still didn't happen.

Of course Alex was famous for his Bible studies!  He had about three per week; one on a weekday morning; one during an evening; one on Sunday morning early.  He called them "Bible 101," and made them pretty close to the equivalent of a college level Bible study course.  The Herrons heard about them and decided to visit.  But first they went to see Alex.

"Reverend," they said, "we are long-time members of our church and we don't want people there to get all out of joint about our coming here.  But we've asked our minister repeatedly to start a Bible study group, and he procrastinates!  He always promises he will, but nothing happens.  We even offered to organize one, but he said he would do it himself.  We can't wait any longer."

"However, we would like to keep our coming here confidential to keep from causing any waves in our home church.

May we attend your two weekday sessions without you informing anyone about our attendance?"

Alex agreed.

As time went by, the Herrons really got involved. Sometimes Alex and the Bible class would study a passage that Alex planned to use as the text for his sermon the following Sunday. On those occasions, the Herrons would skip their own services to attend. Pretty soon their Sunday morning attendance became a regular thing. They decided that they wanted to transfer their membership. However, they went about it in a less than well-planned manner.

One Sunday they went back to their home church, waited for the minister to come out of his study before morning worship began, and waylaid him in the hall. "Allen," they said, "we've something to tell you. We've decided to transfer our membership to the church where Alex is pastor. We've been attending Bible study classes there and we think that is where we belong. So we'll be asking for our letter of transfer."

I'm sure that put Allen in a beautiful mood to begin worship that day! The Herrons were, as I have said, key members. They were large givers and leaders in many committees. Their departure was a serious blow.

Monday morning, in a rage, Allen sat down and dashed off a letter to Alex. It was the kind of letter one should write, retain, and then discard. He didn't; he mailed it immediately. In it he told Alex that in all of his career he had never met a minister who was so unethical; to steal his members; never to inform him that they had been attending; never to tell them to go back to their home church; never to intervene! He vented his wrath in the letter.

At that point I got a phone call from Alex and was asked to come to see him. I found he was angry. Showing me the letter, he remarked, "Did you ever see such an insulting letter? He didn't phone me; he did not hear the circumstances. I had been told to keep their presence here confidential. Never did I suggest they become members; that was a surprise to me too."

**69**

"Are you going to answer him?" I inquired.

"Not on your life. I want nothing to do with him! Anyone who would send me a letter like that doesn't deserve my attention."

This was disturbing. Two brother pastors, both fine people, estranged. I hoped I could intervene.

I suggested to both that we meet, with me present. Both declined.

I went to see Allen. "Allen," I explained, "Alex had been told to keep the Herrons' attendance in his Bible study confidential. He was bound by that promise."

"Hogwash!" Allen exploded. "The minute they came into worship on Sunday morning, their presence was no longer confidential; it was public knowledge. He could have called me right then!"

I relayed that response to Alex. "What nonsense," he responded. "If their presence in my sanctuary was public knowledge, so was their absence in his! He didn't need a phone call from me in order to call them and tell them they had been missed!"

Nothing I said mattered. I knew both of these men. Although Allen had procrastinated in beginning Bible studies, I knew him as a fine pastor and preacher and one deeply involved in the community. He was an advocate for the poor. He had his fine points, as did Alex.

Both were explosive by temperament. Both, usually, got over their anger quickly. If I could only get them together!

"Alex," I pleaded, "if anyone should be able to understand that nasty letter Allen sent to you, it should be you! That is the way you might have reacted yourself in similar circumstances! You understand people who fly off the handle but don't hold a grudge."

"Just forget it, Doc. I don't see him often anyway; let it go."

I couldn't let it go. But I didn't know what else to do. So it just became a matter of prayer, and I found no other tactics to try.  Maybe time would help.

A few months later I got a phone call from Alex.  "Doc, you sly fox!  You set it up, didn't you?"

I didn't have a clue what he was talking about, and said so.

"You know very well what I mean!  Arranging for Allen and I to be roommates at the conference?"

My mouth fell open in amazement.  "You and Allen roomed together?  Without killing each other?"

There was a pause.  "You really didn't know?"

"No, I didn't know!  What happened?"

"Well, when I got to the conference I was assigned to a certain room.  When I opened the door, there was Allen!  Out of all the people there, we had been paired as roommates by somebody!"

"What happened?"

"Well, I guess neither one of us wanted to be the one to walk out.  So I unpacked, and we talked briefly.  Then we went to the opening dinner, and sat together.  That night, in the room, we talked over the speech we had heard."

"The funny thing is, the next day we found ourselves purposefully sitting together at the meetings!  He's really a pretty nice guy."

"But what about your controversy?  Did he apologize, or did you?"

"We didn't talk about that at all.  I guess that is past history now anyway.  But we just found we enjoyed one another's company."

"Doc, are you sure this wasn't arranged?"

"Oh, I'm sure it was arranged!  But not by me!"

# Hospital Horrors
### and
## Hallelujahs

# 1

## *Ramming Around*

It was easy to slam the ladder up against the house and scamper up it!  It was also easy to leap off of it onto the roof and scurry around emptying all the gutters from their accumulated gunk collected during the early fall.  The leaves and walnuts had to go!  I had a lot to do; once this was done I wanted to mow the yard and then race to a meeting at one of our churches.  Hurry, hurry!  But I was going to make it.

I tossed down the last load of leaves, smiled, and bounded onto the ladder.  To my horror, it slipped!  And I already had both feet on it.  I made a mad grab for the gutter, missed, and hit the ground with a thud.  Looking up, I saw that my shoe had come off; the sole was pointed toward me.  Then I realized that my foot was still in it.

Somehow my ankle had gotten between two steps of the aluminum ladder, and I had almost amputated my foot.

It didn't feel too bad . . . yet.  I shouted, "Help!" a few times to no avail; nobody was home and the neighbors didn't hear.  Since the garage door was open I realized I could crawl through the garage, into the house, and reach a phone.  I did that, dragging my foot which was hanging loosely by some remaining flesh to my leg.  I dialed 911, asked for help, hung up, heard the volunteer ambulance siren begin to sound, and thought, "Now what?"

I phoned Betty and told her, "When you come home I

probably won't be here. I think I'll be in the hospital by then." I explained what had happened.

Betty knows I'm a fainter. "Did you faint?" she asked. Later she told me she was sorry she put that thought into my head. It is funny how a smashed finger or thumb can keel me right over, but this more serious accident didn't. After she hung up she called a friend who was a nurse, got the name of the best doctor for broken bones around, and called him to meet me at the hospital. By the time I got there, he was waiting for me. So was she!

I noticed that the nurses took one look at my foot and grimaced. "Doctor, can you fix it?" I asked. He replied reassuringly that he could, but said first they needed to x-ray me. "Why?" I wondered. "I think I know what is broken!"

"Ah, yes," he responded, "but maybe something else is broken too!" I hadn't thought of that.

"But before you put me under," I said, "I have to make a phone call."

"Don't be ridiculous," the doctor answered. "Your work can wait. You've had a serious accident."

"But I really have to make a call!" I said. "Please!"

The doctor tried to ignore me, but Betty could see I was getting frantic. "Give me just a minute with him," she intervened. "He'll be more at peace if you do."

The doctor shrugged, and I quickly explained to Betty that tomorrow morning I was supposed to fly to New York City, go to Grand Central Terminal, and meet the train. An eighty-year-old woman from Massachusetts was coming to a meeting; and I had faithfully promised her that when she got off the train I'd be standing there. I had to let her know.

Betty said she'd make the phone call and tell her not to come; she'd let everybody know. Now I could put my mind on the business at hand.

"Doctor, I'm a walker. I want to be fixed so I can really walk. I don't mean to the house from the car; I mean mountain trails. That's what I do."

**73**

"Trust me," he said. I knew I was in good hands.

"Lord, here I go," I silently prayed. "Be with me." And thus my hospital ordeal began.

# 2

## *How Long Did You Say?*

After I woke up, the doctor explained that my foot had been nearly amputated. They had a drain inserted to try to keep an infection from setting in. The bone had been exposed, and I had dragged it across the dirty garage floor. I'd be there awhile.

"How long?" I asked. When he said perhaps a couple of weeks, I knew that was impossible.

"Doctor!" I exploded. I have fifteen meetings in seven days. People count on me all over this region. I am the only staff person to visit and counsel with sixty-two congregations. I can't possibly be here that long!"

Later, after a four-month stay, I would gladly have gone back to his original offer!

Neither of us knew then what was ahead. "You really have no choice," he said. "You can't walk; this will take awhile. You'll find the world goes on without you."

How humbling! But true. Years later, somewhat facetiously, I told people that I thought that people couldn't get along without me; later I found out they said, "Oh, have you been away?"

The problem was an infection. Sure enough, I developed one. They had to operate again, clean it out, start over with anti-biotics. This delayed things a bit. I was back to square one.

As days went by, I noticed the doctor was not pleased by

my blood tests. The infection was continuing. There was another operation, then another. They tried medicine after medicine. Nothing seemed to slow the infection which had entered the bone. I had osteomyelitis, "Is this serious?" I asked.

"Yes, very. Especially because we can't seem to discover what kind of infection you have."

Let me shorten my "horror story." Altogether there were six operations. They left the ankle spread open, and cleaned it out every few hours, which hurt. Finally a bacteriologist identified a rare fungus, risopus. "What is that?"

"Bread mold!" the doctor said. "It is not very serious in bread; it is bad news in a bone. Very unusual! There have been only five known cases of this in human beings before."

"What happened to them?" I asked. It was not reassuring that he refused to answer!

"Oh Lord, help! I'm too young to die! I don't want my leg amputated. Help!"

A few days later the doctor returned to tell me that there was one medicine that might kill the fungus. I would have to have it dripped into my veins for several hours each day. It did have side effects.

"Such as?"

"Well, it could destroy your kidneys. You might have to be on dialysis.."

"Amputate!" I ordered. "I could live with one foot but I don't want to live on a machine!"

"Now, let's just try it," he answered. "We'll monitor your kidneys every day. If they start to fail, we'll stop. It's worth a try."

I agreed, and the long treatment began. During my time in the hospital I had some adventures, met some people, and had some thoughts I never would have had otherwise. I'm not ready to say that being there was a good thing, but some good things happened. Since I was in a room with two beds, roommates came and went while I stayed on and on! I'll never forget some of them.

# 3

## Roommates and Visitors

They came and went, but I stayed! During my four-month ordeal, I had a variety of interesting roommates and visitors.

The first roommate, I am convinced, was running a bookie operation from his bed! He had a badly fractured leg which did not slow down his thinking or his talking by telephone. I don't know what was going on for sure, but conversations that I overheard went something like this:

"Okay, Joe, you're down for twenty on three."

"Bill, are you in this week? No, that's up to you; I can't tell you. Not a bad choice; Billy will come by to pick it up."

He checked out a couple of days after I arrived, so I never knew for sure, but what else could it be?

My second roommate was an older man who seemed a bit sullen. He wouldn't talk much. After the third day the nurses came in, pulled the curtains, and loaded him into a portable bed and swept him away. A little later his son came in, very apologetically, to explain that his Dad had insisted upon being moved to another room because I had stolen his false teeth.

"I know that's crazy," he said. "He probably left them on his lunch tray. But he can't get any peace; he's afraid to go to sleep with you in the room. Please forgive us for moving him to another room."

I was flabbergasted! What in the world would I want

77

with his false teeth? I was glad the son had explained, and understood the problem was in his father's mind.

My third roommate was a blessed relief at first. He was quiet most of the time, but talkative when we were both in the mood. He seemed eager to get acquainted. One day he asked, "I notice you read your Bible each day. Do you belong to a church?"

"Oh yes," I said. I'm a member of the Disciples of Christ. What about you?"

"I'm a Jehovah's Witness," he answered.

God have mercy! And I can't escape; I'm confined to my bed! I was afraid I would be subjected to twenty-four hour per day witnessing from this point forward.

It didn't happen. I guess he had problems of his own right now. It taught me again not to be so quick to generalize from earlier bad experiences.

Then came Fred! I'll never forget Fred.

When Fred moved in, I discovered I was sharing a room with a man who never stopped talking. He even talked back to the reporters on television. If the weather forecaster said, "It may rain today," Fred would reply, "No kidding!" After each sentence, Fred joined the conversation.

His voice was loud, but he called my name even louder. Whatever he said was often followed by, "Isn't that right, CHARLIE?"

At night I'd have to say, "Fred, I'm going to sleep now." Maybe ten minutes later, after I stopped answering questions, he'd finally tone down to a few mumbled comments to himself and give me some peace until, too soon, the next morning I'd hear, "Good morning, CHARLIE!"

After one of my multiple operations, I didn't feel very well and Fred's incessant talking was bothering me. "Fred," I said, "I don't mean to be rude, but I just can't talk."

"Don't worry, CHARLIE! I understand. You just rest, and I'll go ahead and talk to you."

When Fred finally checked out, I gave a sigh of relief.

Finally, peace and quiet. A few hours later, my bedside phone rang and I picked it up to hear a familiar voice.

"CHARLIE! How are you? I miss you. Do you have time to talk?"

"Sorry, Fred, I can't talk now. I miss you too. Goodbye."

I did miss him, but it was a good miss.

Jerry was pathetic. He was a nice older man who didn't see well and who often needed to go to the bathroom. Neither of us could get out of bed. He would say, "Doc, where is that urinal of mine?"

"Right beside your bed, Jerry. It's hanging on the side rail."

He would lower his hand, shakily groping for it in the wrong place.

"No, Jerry, higher up. Now toward the front. Too far! Back a little. Now down."

"Never mind, Doc, it's too late now anyhow."

But Jerry solved the problem. I noticed he'd quit asking where the urinal was, and I understood why when one day when the nurse came to remove his tray after a meal she said, "Jerry, is that what I think it is in your coffee cup?"

Bill was a deacon in the church to which I belonged, a bachelor who lived with two other brothers in a farm house just outside town. He had always been pleasant but I'd never had any real social contact with him. Then one day he came walking into my room with a chess set under his arm.

"Doc, your wife tells me you like chess."

"Yes I do, Bill. Why?"

"Well, I came to play chess with you."

So we played, three games. He was slightly better than I, but not so much so that the games weren't interesting. He won two of three.

"I'll be back next week," he said. "Might as well leave the chess set here so as not to carry it."

Bill was my faithful visitor; I'll never stop appreciating

his concern and his way of helping me pass the time and feel loved.

I had other visitors as well. One Hispanic couple came from a couple of hundred miles away. The husband played the guitar while his wife sang to me: "The Spirit of the Lord is here; I can feel his presence o so near," until I was moved to tears.

One local pastor made a call I could have done without. "My God, Doc!" he exploded. "If this had happened to me I think I'd just jump right out that window!"

The local Presbyterian minister came faithfully, making helpful pastoral calls. I was on the prayer list in his church. He did all of this fully knowing I would never be a prospective member since I had my own ministry with the Disciples. I realized again how the Church really is one and our divisions are so artificial.

Our Regional Moderator was marvelous. She set out to visit every church in the Region during my long incapacity and pretty nearly made it. She even preached when asked! She truly functioned as the Regional Minister while I couldn't do it.

One day she dropped by, laughing. She'd been to our church in Vermont, and preached there. "I always knew New Englanders were supposed to be people of few words," she said, "but I didn't realize how few. After I preached I stood at the door to shake hands. One person shook my hand and said, 'I enjoyed your sermon.' The next one in line simply added ...very much!' "

I've saved Uncle Joe for last. Because of his age and personality I called him "Uncle," especially after I learned his relatives all said that and he seemed to like it. Uncle Joe became my roommate after I'd been there awhile and had several operations without much success. He was a saintly looking white-haired gentleman with serious health problems. Both feet had been amputated previously due to severe diabetes. Now he had heart problems. We had some beautiful talks. One day he collapsed and was rushed to the emergency room. He recovered, but this time they put him into a private room across the hall. I missed our talks.

Then one day a nurse wheeled him into my room. Sitting in his wheel chair, he explained. "Doc, I heard you were going in for another operation tomorrow so I asked them to bring me here to pray with you."

Now Uncle Joe knew I was a protestant minister, and he didn't make any attempt to convert me to his faith, but he did not hesitate to be who he was either. He pressed a small medal of the Virgin Mary into my hand. "Keep this, Doc," he said. "It brought me through my operation and it will help you."

I was touched. "Uncle Joe, this won't have the same meaning for me that it does for you, exactly, but I'll treasure it because it is from you."

"I want to pray with you, Doc," he continued. Of course I agreed. He grasped his rosary and explained, "When I pray I have to pray in Ukrainian; that's the only way I can do this. Okay?"

Of course it was okay. While he prayed I watched his face. There was no doubt about the sincerity and the love he felt, and no doubt in my mind that God was hearing every word.

Two days later the nurses told me that he had been checked out of the hospital, but since I was asleep he had insisted that they stop his wheelchair just outside my door and let him pray for me one more time before he left.

About one week later I learned that he had died. I wrote down the facts of my visits with Uncle Joe on tear stained pages and sent them to his children. I was told later that the priest read the letter during his funeral.

Uncle Joe's influence lives on in my life. After my eventual discharge, a neighbor lady developed cancer. She was Roman Catholic. My first reaction was to tell her that I would pray for her. Then I remembered Uncle Joe. "He didn't say he would pray for me. He did it!" I reminded myself.

I didn't want to be accused of trying to steal a member of another church, but Uncle Joe's example gave me the

**81**

courage to go call and say, "I know you are Catholic, but we both worship the same God, and I wonder if you would like for me to pray with you while I'm here."

"Oh, yes!" she said, and we did.

Thank you, Uncle Joe, for making me a more courageous Christian.

# 4

## *Day After Day*

Time in the hospital, for me, dragged by. Encounters with other people, however, helped! When you are any place for a long period of time, it seems, interesting things happen.

A young minister came to see me. He seemed a bit ill at ease; I think he hadn't made too many hospital calls. Perhaps that wasn't it; perhaps he was thinking that as his Regional Minister I might think it was presumptuous of him to come minister to me. That certainly wasn't how I was feeling! I was not a regional minister there at all. I was just old Doc, very frail, worried and depressed.

As he got ready to leave I asked, "Won't you pray with me?"

He looked surprised. "You want me to?"

"I surely do."

I told him about my first church and my call, at about age twenty-five, on an older parishioner. I considered the man to be more like a father than anything else, and I wondered if he would think this young seminary student had anything to offer. I asked him if he wanted me to pray.

He looked startled. "Of course! You're my minister!"

"You always can assume," I told him, "that people in the hospital will want your prayers. Occasionally somebody will say 'no,' but ninety-nine percent of the time they'll be glad. When I call, I usually offer to pray for the person in the next bed also if they wish, and almost always they gratefully accept."

"People here," I continued, "are clinging to their faith and hope and eager for any help they can get!"

So he prayed, a good prayer! And I'll bet he does pray in the future for people too.

His feeling ill at ease reminded me of my own first hospital call. I was a young intern, working under a senior minister who had been called out of town. While he was away a member of our church went to the hospital, and I realized I should go visit.

She was as elderly lady who had been hospitalized several times before. I thought how discouraged she must be to be going back to the hospital one more time! I decided my main duty must be to give her words of encouragement.

When I entered her room, however, she looked much better than I expected. She was sitting up in bed, appearing to be ready to be discharged. "It will be easy to encourage her," I thought, but my words were ill chosen.

I blurted out, "Well! You don't look like you'll be here much longer!"

She gave me a withering stare and mumbled, "I'm going home, if that's what you mean!"

One of my frequent visitors was an African American pastor named Maynard. One day when he called, my son happened to arrive at the very same time. My roommate evidently thought my son looked like me, and asked, "Is that your son?"

"Yes he is," I answered.

At that moment Maynard, who has a great sense of humor, addressed my roommate, interjecting: "No, not him! Me!"

My roommate began to laugh at the idea that he was my son. Suddenly Maynard grew very stern. "Why is that funny to you? Don't you think I look like my father?"

My poor roommate didn't know what to say! I tried to get him off the hook by changing the subject.

Of course I encountered a great variety of personalities

among the nurses as well. One served as a private nurse for awhile for one of my roommates. He would praise her at great length as the best nurse he had ever had in all of his hospitalizations. One day, after she left the room, I asked, "William, do you really think she is that great; better than any other you ever had?"

"Heck no," he answered, "but I think I get better service that way."

I think he just marked himself as a hypocrite.

I can't praise nurses enough though. Many of them, despite overwork and too much to do, show amazing compassion and empathy for the patients. In fact, I have a friend who is a minister but also returned to school to become a registered nurse as well. He said he wanted to be able to help people with direct physical aid as well as in spiritual matters.

A newspaper reporter was intrigued by a minister returning to school to become a nurse. I guess the reporter felt it might have been more normal for a nurse to become a minister. So the reporter asked him, "Why didn't you decide to become a doctor?"

My friend responded explosively: "Because I'm interested in healing, not in power!"

The reporter wrote a story and quoted that remark. I'm sure it went up on bulletin boards in schools of nursing everywhere.

In my experience, I couldn't have had more compassionate doctors as well. We always have to avoid the generalizations. But the nurses are there for much longer periods of time and get involved with the patients.

There was one person on our floor suffering from an incurable and desperately painful illness. I remarked to a nurse, one day, that I did not think it was wrong, in such cases, for a person to have the right to decide to end life. "We make responsible decisions under God all our days," I explained. "We decide about a career, about whom to marry, about how many children to have, about what to do with our time and money. Is it so different to decide that the time to end suffering has come?"

She said, "I agree with you."

I was amazed. "I thought the medical profession took a very hard line against that."

"Not the nurses," she said, "because we deal with those cases."

Sometimes the nurses may be better equipped to minister than the pastors. If they do it as a ministry, I give them credit. One of our pastors, a confirmed bachelor, had a tough experience trying to make a constructive call.

Jerry was a round, pink-faced man, but when he came into my room his face wasn't pink; it was bright red. "I just had the most terrible experience, Doc!" he confessed.

"What happened?"

"Well, I had just called on one of my members and was starting to go when she asked me to go down the hall to another room to visit a friend of her's, whom I didn't know. So I did."

"And what happened?"

"Well, before I could say anything, the lady in her bed said, 'Come in! Come in! I've been waiting for you!'

"I guessed my parishioner had told her I'd call, so I did.

"But then she suddenly pulled down the covers and pulled up her night shirt to show me a rash all over her breast. 'Look at this rash!' she said.

"Before I could answer, she pulled up the bottom of her nightgown to show me the same rash, uh, down below.

"My face must have turned color because she suddenly said, 'You are a doctor, aren't you?'

" 'No!,' I said, 'I'm not!' and I fled! I'm still shaking!"

Hospital calling can be hazardous.

There are doctors, nurses, ministers, and friends who do wonderful deeds of love and compassion; there are others who just do their duty, if that. Most know their skills and limitations; some don't. Some patients know how to assert their own rights, stay in control of their own destiny, but act courteously and considerately to those who work there; others don't. Life in the hospital is like life outside. You meet all kinds of people.

But, as Will Rogers once said, you have to get a few laughs along the way. They keep you going.

# 5

## *Doctors and Nurses*

When my doctor told me that they had finally identified the fungus that was destroying my ankle bone, and then explained that the only medicine which might kill it might also kill my kidneys, I was a trifle upset!  My first reaction, of course, was to order, "Amputate!  I can live without a foot, but I really don't want to be hooked up to a machine."

The doctor had calmed me, reassuring me that they would monitor my kidneys daily.  If they started to fail they would discontinue the treatment.  Thinking about that later, though, I realized, "And then what?  If this is the only medicine that will work, and I can't take it, then what?"  I thought I knew what.

A couple of days later the doctor reappeared.  "The nurses tell me you are a little depressed," he offered.  "We know that patients heal better if they stay positive and jovial.  I want you to see a psychiatrist."

"Doctor!" I exclaimed.  "If you tell a person his kidneys may fail and he may be on dialysis, and he reacts with cheer and joy, I think he might need a psychiatrist!  But if you want me to talk to one, send him in.  I'll cooperate with anything you suggest."

A couple of days later a psychiatrist appeared at my door, introduced himself, and came in to sit at my bedside.

"Watching television any?" he asked.

Actually, I had been watching baseball games each afternoon. The World Series was on, and that helped me spend a few hours each day.

"Which team are you for?"

"Neither, I just watch the game. When Buffalo gets a major league I'll be for them."

"Did you watch yesterday? What did you think of that disputed call?"

I told him I thought the call was unfair, but accidentally so.

And so it went. We talked about baseball for most of the hour. When he left I wondered, "How much did my insurance company pay for that?"

How fast we judge! The psychiatrist knew exactly what he was doing; namely, testing to see if I could put my mind on other things rather than my own condition. He reported to the doctor that my level of depression was about normal under my circumstances. If I had not been able to concentrate on baseball, he would have come to another conclusion.

But then a nurse's aide came to call. She was a small African American woman whom I had seen frequently. But this time she looked at me with a little more attention than usual and said, "You read your Bible a lot; why don't you try the one hundred and twenty third Psalm?"

I knew what she meant, of course. The twenty-third Psalm is such a favorite: "The Lord is my Shepherd, I shall not want." My mind raced ahead to "Even though I walk through the valley of the shadow of death, I will fear no evil, for Thou art with me...."

"I know what you mean, the twenty-third Psalm," I replied. "Thank you, I do read it."

She looked at me as though she had to explain the obvious. "Yes, the twenty-third Psalm is good too. But I said the one hundred and twenty third Psalm. That's what you need now I think."

When she left the room I couldn't wait to look up the one hundred twenty-third Psalm to see what it said. And I found: "As the eyes of servants look to the hand of their master, as the eyes of a maid to the hand of her mistress, so our eyes look to the Lord our God until he has mercy upon us." (verse 2)

"Oh Lord, my eyes do look to you! How long until you have mercy?"

And then a quiet inner voice said, "My presence IS my mercy. Whatever happens, you're safe with Me."

Of course I still wanted to be healed, and out of the hospital, but something happened to me then. Prayer couldn't be begging. Prayer just had to be surrendering and trusting myself to God. It changed me. And I've been changed, I think, ever since.

I thanked the nurse; I'm not sure the thanks I gave her were ever adequate. If she ever reads this, I hope she'll know what that simple visit of her's meant to me.

Of course there were other nurses with different perspectives. One came in for long talks that were really counseling. One was so indifferent that I finally had to complain. She was the exception. They were all overworked, and I think she had just lost her sense of "calling." One gave the world's best back rubs at night. And then there was Jodie.

Jodie was young and cute and innocent and very concerned that I was in the hospital for so long! One day, in an embarrassed way, she made a suggestion. "Doc, you have been here for months! That is hard on a married man. I think we could arrange for your wife to pay a conjugal visit. We could keep people out of the room for awhile. Shall I work on that?"

I could imagine Betty's reaction, especially with someone else just across the room behind a curtain. "Jodie, I do thank you; you are really concerned for me, but I'll be okay. We'll be together again soon." I hoped that was the truth! I was so tired of the hospital.

When I think how difficult it was to be confined to one room, without outside air, for four months, then I marvel at the endurance of hostages in Iran who were kept for years in terrible conditions by people who were not trying to help them, but hurt them! My problems pale into insignificance. But when they are one's own problems, they are very large at the time.

Jodie was still worried. "Well, maybe I could bring you a Playboy Magazine at least," she offered!

After I was finally out of the hospital Betty and I set up a social hour at our home and invited all the doctors and nurses who had helped me. Many came! And I went to the Presbyterian Church in my neighborhood so that I could publicly thank the people there for their many visits and prayers.

When I think back on my hospital incarceration now, I feel the way many people who have been in basic training in the armed forces seem to feel. They say, "I never would want to do that again! But I learned a lot." I guess I feel that way too.

Isn't it interesting that when we exercise physically, with some exhaustion and pain, our bodies get stronger. We don't help our muscles or general health by resting. Spiritually it seems to be the same; it is during the difficult days when we grow closer to God. We don't want those difficult days back, but we're glad for the people we met and the things we learned when we had them.

# 6

## *Christmas in the Hospital*

Was I still going to be there on Christmas Day? Yes I was!

Betty was doing everything she could to help me. Not only did she have all the work at home and with the kids, but she came to see me daily. Often she brought food; the hospital food was good but repetitious and after several weeks I was so tired of the same menu she started bringing me some meals from outside.

One of my greatest complaints against the hospital was that they wouldn't agree for me to go outside for short periods of time. The doctor decided it would do me good to be outdoors for an hour or two a day, but the hospital administration said the moment I went out the door I was discharged. I was ready to do it anyway, but then learned that my insurance company might decide if I could do that I was now an outpatient. So I had to keep breathing the disinfectant-tainted air and long to just feel the wind on my face.

Now it was Christmas; what a sad time to be there.

We had a Christmas tree at home even though I wasn't there to help. Betty and the boys had picked one out but when they got home it was too tall to fit into the room. She asked one of my sons to shorten it. He topped it!

Christmas Day, in addition to Betty's visit, two single friends came and spent the entire day with me! I was so touched. They could have been at parties or with friends, but instead they just settled in for a long visit with me. We talked, ate together, watched television, told Christmas stories. How much it meant to me! They did help the day pass by.

They did more than that! They reminded me again of the meaning of Christmas. The gift they gave me, the gift of their presence and love, didn't come in a box with a ribbon on the top. It came in person, in the flesh, and it reminded me again of the power of love. God so loved the world that he gave his only Son...

They gave me Christmas.

## *Do Your School Work!*

There was another problem with being in the hospital so long!  I was getting hopelessly behind on my schoolwork!

Some time ago I had enrolled in a Doctor of Ministry program in New York Theological Seminary.  This was a special program for people in professions such as mine; denominational executives, ecumenical officers, etc.  It met for one or two days of intensive study each month.  In between sessions there were books to read, papers to write, projects to perform.  After 1 ½ years of studies, there would be a major project and a paper.

I had discovered that I could manage to be in New York City for my work at the right times so as to stay over for the study sessions.  My Board was very supportive of this continuing education effort and I was off to a good start.

When I missed one month's classes, I was dismayed.  I wrote a letter of apology, asked for make up reading and notes, and assured the professors that I would be back soon.

Then I missed the second month.  That was a disaster, I felt.  Once more I dashed off a letter of apology.  I received a response that I was not to worry, just get well, and they'd see me the following month.

The third month came; I was still in the hospital.  The phone beside my bed rang; it was my professor!  I knew what he wanted for sure.  No doubt he was going to tell me to drop out of the program and try it again some future year.

"How are you feeling?" he asked. I told him that I was confined to bed with an ankle spread open to the bone and tubes dripping medicine into my veins. I couldn't go anywhere. But there was nothing wrong with my mind; I could read and write and talk.

"I do understand if you want me to drop out of the program," I managed to say despite the agony I felt. "After all, I'm missing too much."

"You are missing too much," he countered, "but we don't want you to drop out. Two of us are thinking of flying to Buffalo, coming to the hospital, and giving you a make up session. Are you up to that?"

I was thunderstruck. Come all the way here to spend time with me? But the cost was a problem.

"That is a wonderful offer," I replied, "but frankly, I don't think I can afford two round trip plane ticket fares right now."

"No, no," he replied, "we wouldn't charge you for that. The seminary will cover it."

I could hardly believe it. "Come, by all means!" I urged.

And they did. And they had no mercy! They were tough, maybe even tougher than in the classroom. By the time they left, I was exhausted. Caught up. And happy!

It was also time for our Regional Executive Committee to meet. The chairperson of our Board had learned of the professors' visit, so she had an idea to follow the same example. Without my knowing it, she contacted the hospital administration and discovered that there was a waiting room that would accommodate the nine members of that committee plus myself. Then she appeared in my doorway one day to say, "Doc, it's time for the Executive Committee to meet. We can't wait any longer for you to get out of the hospital."

"I know that," I replied, "so you will have to meet without me. Maybe I can help prepare the agenda."

"You can help do that too," she said, "but we want to meet with you.'

"I know, I know!  But what can I do?"

She smiled.  "Guess what?  We've arranged to have the meeting here.  If you can meet your professors and do class work, I guess you can have a meeting and do church work!"

She was right.  Work never felt so good.

People were good to me.  Even while I was dismayed over my imprisonment and worried about my future health, they managed to include me in their lives and go out of their way to keep me involved.  For that I will always be grateful.

# 8

## *Going Home at Last*

Finally, the doctor came by to say, "We think we have the infection licked. You're doing very well."

"So I can go home soon?"

"Well, don't forget we have to put your ankle back together first. And that brings us to a time for decision."

"What do you mean?"

"You don't have a lot of ankle joint left; the fungus ate up a lot of bone. We're thinking of fusing it, taking bone from your pelvic area to replace the joint. If we do that, you won't be able to bend your ankle anymore but you probably won't have any pain and it maximizes the chance that the fungus won't reoccur."

"What's the other choice?"

"We could just set your ankle without fusing it and see how you do. You might always have a lot of pain there, but if it is too bad we could fuse it later."

"What are the odds? What would you do?"

The doctor sighed. "Oh, for the good old days when doctors just made decisions; now we have to let you know everything and decide everything! Never mind what I would do. I can't tell you the odds, and I certainly can't say the fungus would never come back. If you shake salt from a shaker into a shag rug and then go gather it up, can you guarantee me you got all the salt?"

"But Doctor! I don't know!"

"Then why don't you go get a second opinion. You can take all the x-rays and charts. If a second doctor says what I've said, you'll be reassured. If he says something different, I need to hear it."

"What doctor?"

"Oh, no! Then you'll think he just wants to agree with me. You choose the doctor."

I liked my doctor! He was very confident, very caring, and I would have trusted his opinion on anything.

Betty talked with her nurse friend, and soon I was on my way to Buffalo to see another doctor. I was so happy to be out of the hospital, even briefly. "Stop the car, Betty, just let me roll down the window, breathe the air, look at the trees!"

Doctor number two was not as democratic. After looking at the x-rays he said, "Man, you have no choice; there isn't enough joint here left to save. Go get it fused!"

I wondered how difficult it would be to walk with a foot that wouldn't bend. I also wondered how people would feel who had been praying for me if they found out I had chosen the fusion. But I felt peace about it as the right choice.

In retrospect, I'm glad. At my age I don't have to leap to shoot basketballs or spike volleyballs, and I walk fine. It is tough to put my foot into boots, however! When you can't tuck your toes down it makes a difference!

I went into the final operation just as into the others. "Oh Lord, here I go! Help me know I'm in your hands."

After the fusion, I was fitted with a contraption beyond my belief. There were pins inserted into my foot, near the big toe, and into the leg above the ankle, with crossbars linking them. I looked like something out of science fiction. People would look at this contraption, realize the pins went right into the flesh and into the bone, and grimace!

But now I could go home! I was to continue taking the fungus killing medicine there, but I could manage that. Bags of the medicine were delivered to the house, put into the freezer, and I was to use one each day for several weeks.

The nurse explained that I had to do it carefully, not get any air in the line, not get any kinks, or I could maybe kill myself. Betty exploded: "This is the man who rams around and falls off ladders; you're going to trust him to do this by himself?"

"Don't worry, Betty," I assured her. "I have a lot at stake in doing this right.

Betty had to go to work, so the next morning she put a little bell beside my bed, smiled, and told me if I needed anything to ring it and she would come. Then she went to work! I rang the bell, but found it not too effective! Actually, I was fine, except for being bored. I was so wired up to my dripping medicine for several hours that I couldn't go anywhere.

At last the treatments ended. The doctor was very pleased. "You've made medical history," he told me. "I'm going to write an article about this for the medical journals."

"Do I get royalties?" He just smiled.

"Since you decided to have your ankle fused, we removed not only the infected area but a wide area around it," he said. "I don't think you'll have any more trouble. But we'll keep an eye on you for awhile. But now, we have to get those pins out of your leg."

"Oh no! Another operation!"

"Heavens no!" he laughed. "That's nothing; it's painless."

So I went to the hospital, on the assigned day, to have the "chute" taken out of my chest into which they'd been dripping medicine for months, and the pins taken out of my leg, all at the same time.

The doctor who had installed the chute had told me that wouldn't hurt either, he didn't think. I wondered what he meant by "think."

"Oh, everyone else that had one was terminal and died," he explained, "so I've never taken one out before."

It hurt but it was fast. Then it was time for the pins to come out. My alarm antenna went up when I heard the doctor ask the nurse for "a drill." To my amazement, the pins unscrewed in much the same way that a mechanic removes nuts from a wheel before taking it off my car. "Whirrrrrr!" and a pin pops out. As each of the four pins was removed, I yelled, but by the time I had yelled it was out. I sat up on the bed and looked at the bloody sheet near my ankle.

"See, that didn't hurt!" the doctor smiled. What do you do with these people that tell you things don't hurt when they do?

But it was over. After doing my work on crutches for a long time, back pack as a suitcase when I traveled, I finally was pronounced "done" and not needing future visits. What a relief.

But I had had an experience that changed me. Now I know what it feels like to be in the hospital bed rather than the minister making the call. Now I know how much a card or a visit means; more than I could ever have dreamed. Now I know how it feels to be surrounded and lifted up by prayers.

The doctor told me I had been a good patient, that I endured surgery nicely and had responded well. "Because of prayers," I assured him. I don't know if he believed that, but I do.

God worked through doctors, nurses, friends, and family. But God did it. And when I hear that someone else is sick or in need, I hope I can respond half as well as many people did for me.

It has been several years now since that time. Regularly I still find myself saying, "O Lord, thank you for this beautiful world; I'm so grateful to be outdoors and see it! And thank you for the fresh air. And thank you for people who love me and help me when I need them. Thank you for life!"

At the time I was in the hospital, it seemed that ordeal would never end. But it did. Everything passes, change occurs. But God's presence with us is his mercy, and when we find that we have it all.

# *The Wisdom*
## *of*
## *Walter*

# 1

## *It's a Flower to Me*

My grandson, Walter, has always loved flowers! Even before he could pronounce the word, he would beam with delight whenever he saw any kind of flower, and would exclaim, "La las!" Nothing could stop crying or bring a smile as quickly as the sight of any type of blossom. Roses and dandelions were all the same to him; all were beautiful; all were causes for undiluted joy.

So one winter day, when his dad decided to bundle Walter up and take him for a walk, it was not surprising that his first reaction was, "Good! See flowers!" Now that he was two, he could say the word correctly, and the joyful sound of "la las" was fading from his vocabulary, but there was no change in his enthusiasm. Of course his first thought, upon going outdoors, was that another opportunity had occurred in which to see those glorious plants!

"No, Walter, I'm afraid not," his dad warned him. He didn't want him to be too disappointed. "It's winter, it's cold, the flowers have all gone away. They'll come back next summer, but we won't see flowers today."

Walter was not convinced.

Once outdoors, as they began to walk along a pathway through the back yard, Walter suddenly bolted ahead, turned to the side of the path, and grasped a tall weed pod. Brown and dry, the stalk extended upright from the ground for a couple of feet and then bulged in a ball-like shape, perhaps caused by some insect having deposited its eggs there. Since it was brittle, Walter was able to break it off with one try. He came running back to his father with a triumphant grin on his face. "See, Dad! Flower!"

His Dad had to smile at Walter's naivete. "No, I'm afraid not, Walter," he said. "That's just an old weed."

Walter's enthusiasm was not extinguished by this rebuke. He grew thoughtful for a moment, stared at his treasure, and then raised his head to look up at his Dad.

"Well," he said, "It's a flower to me."

Some time ago a gentleman in a nearby community allowed his yard to grow up in all kinds of clover, dandelions, thistles, and milkweed, plus any other plant that happened to take root there. Neighbors complained, reminding him that there was a "weed ordinance" in the community and that people were compelled by law to keep their lawns nicely. He responded that a "weed" is defined as an "unwanted plant," that he wanted all these plants, and that he considered them to be natural land cover.

It is all in the attitude!

Who is to say what is a flower? Are we so programmed by the expectations of others that we must limit our enjoyment to their acceptable boundaries?

Our wise little Walter knew better! "It's a flower to me!" If I enjoy this plant, if I like the look of it with its ball at the top of a brown stem, if I like to see it jutting upward along the side of a path, if I find pleasure in picking it and studying it, even taking it home with me, who can tell me it is just some old weed?

When my friend John died in his mid-forties, I was more angry than sad. John still had children at home and he was needed! A good man, active in his church, living a good life, he was now dead of a brain tumor. It was so unjust. How could anyone have faith in a good God after this tragedy?

Then one day I heard his widow say, "We were so fortunate! We had twenty years of such a happy marriage. I would rather have had these years with John than fifty years of mediocre marriage with anyone else. I am so blessed!"

John, I guess, was a jonquil. Or a daffodil, or crocus. One of those beautiful spring flowers that brighten our days but fade so quickly before the summer is hardly begun. But having him as husband and father was a flower to his wife, no doubt about it. She had learned to say, "It's a flower to me."

When Dick's hand was caught in heavy machinery and he lost most of his fingers, his days of working at that job were done! He told me later, "I was wiped out! I had lost not only my hand, but also my job, my livelihood. But in retrospect it was the best thing that could have happened to me. I used the insurance money to retrain myself in accounting, went back to work for the same company, and later became their business manager! I would still be working on the machinery if it had not been for that accident!"

Another person might have become bitter, but here this man was, actually saying it was the "best thing" that could have happened! In my mind I heard that phrase again. "It's a flower to me!"

And now here I am, getting old, getting gray, with a few creaks and croaks in my bones and joints. Isn't getting old "the pits?" Well, on the other hand, I've lived long enough to become a grandfather. Walter's granddaddy!

And *that's* a flower to me!

## 2

## *These Are Still Peas!*

Now just because our little philosopher is able to take a positive attitude toward life, find joy in common things, and say, "It's a flower to me," you must not think that he is unrealistic. True wisdom finds the balance between reality and idealism and knows how to take a positive but sensible approach to things. This rule of life was brought home to me one day when helping Walter eat his lunch.

I was visiting my grandson during lunch hour, and noted that although he was quite capable, at about age two, of feeding himself unaided, he was not eating very rapidly but dawdling over the meal. Deciding to be a helpful grandfather type, I picked up a spoon and said, "Walter, let me help!" Walter is no fool, and when help is offered it is gladly accepted, especially if associated with some game playing and fun along with the task at hand. We can learn from that too!

I took a spoon, dished up a serving of peas and moved them toward Walter's mouth only to find his lips sealed shut in a tightly drawn line. The spoon poked at his mouth without success; there was no admittance to peas! When I removed the spoon, Walter informed me, "I don't like peas!"

Grandfathers have lots of experience in getting children

**104**

to eat, so I decided the same old tricks that used to work with his mother might still be effective. "Well," I said, "then obviously we'll have to change them into something else for you!" I picked up the spoon of peas and began to make slow circles with it in the air.

"Abra ca dabra!" I intoned. "Magic a dajic! These peas are now transformed, utterly changed, magically altered! They are becoming, becoming..... now *are green diamonds*!"

Green diamonds was a spontaneous expression not considered well in advance. Diamonds may be beautiful, but are hardly appetizing. A little hard for chewing. However, at two, Walter did not know that and the sound of "green diamonds" and his Grandfather's obvious delight in the magic were convincing. He opened his mouth widely and the "green diamonds" went neatly inside.

I smiled at him as I saw him begin to chew the "green diamonds." However, on about the third chew, a cloud passed over Walter's face. His eyes sought and made contact with mine, and I could see the serious expression of doubt and shaken faith they held. Walter has great faith in his grandfather, or perhaps I should say *had* great faith, and the faith was wavering before my eyes.

"Granddaddy!" Walter said, rebukingly. "These are still peas!"

Ah, the wisdom of our young sage! Indeed they were! No clever phrases, no magic words, no hype, could change the fact! Idealism aside, reality prevails here! I think Walter is well on his way to developing the ability to resist commercialism in our society. Just because someone, even a trusted someone, tells you how wonderful something is, it is well to maintain a cautious skepticism until you test it for yourself. Don't be taken in!

While having my car serviced the other day, I wandered into the show room to spend some time looking at newer models. Now, this was not the time for me to buy a new car! The budget won't tolerate it, not just yet. My old jalopy is perfectly fine.  But it is always fun to dream.

The hotshot salesman on duty couldn't leave me in peace, however.  I saw him out of the corner of my eye, headed my way.  Red and white checked jacket, red pants, broad fake smile, glistening teeth like a barracuda, he represented to me the classic image of the type of salesman most to be avoided.  (I don't really know whether or not barracudas have glistening teeth showing through a fake smile, but that's the picture that came to mind.)

"That's just the car for you, Sir!" he screamed at me.  Actually, it was the *last* car I would have considered buying.  I'm not really intending to buy a red sports car; I'm the van or station wagon type!  But he had seen me looking at it, and swooped in for the sale.  "Yes Sir, and are we going to give you a deal!"

"No, no," I replied.  "I'm not going to buy.  I'm just killing time while my car gets serviced."

"Of course you are going to buy today!" said Super-Salesman.  Because I am going to make you a deal you cannot refuse!"

I won't repeat the whole dialogue, since it wore me out, and there is no reason to put others through the same ordeal.  Suffice it to say that despite my continued assertions that I was not interested, did not have sufficient funds, and did not like to be pressured, Super-Salesman never backed off.  Finally he said, "With our special plan you *can* afford it; you can *not* afford to let it go; this car is a gem, and this deal will be so appetizing it will make your mouth water!"

Then I knew I had the right answer for him.  I grinned, looked him in the eye, and said, "These are still peas."

That did it.  He took a step backwards, looked at me strangely, and said, "I beg your pardon?"

Grinning from ear to ear, I persisted.  "That's what I said.  Call it a diamond if you want, Mister.  *These are still peas*!"

That got rid of him.  I doubt if he captured the wisdom

of the philosophy; he may have thought he was dealing with a mentally unstable person. But I knew his so-called deal was unappetizing, regardless of what he called it. They were still peas. And I told him so.

It worked! Thank you, Walter!

# 3

## *Lots of Imagination*

I didn't really finish my story of feeding Walter peas. After he tried chewing the "green diamonds" I had magically created and had remorsefully concluded that they were still peas, I persisted. To my shame, I was so determined to outmaneuver my grandson that I tried again.

I said, "Well, Walter, we'll just have to try again, and use lots and lots of imagination!" I didn't know if Walter would go for it, but he decided to give me another chance. But this time he would be involved himself.

"Make them green circles, Granddaddy," he requested. No more of those green diamonds, please!

This time I took the spoonful of peas in slower circles while intoning, "Abra ca dabra, magic a dajic, kapow! kapooy! These peas are now *green circles*!" As I put them into Walter's mouth I warned him, "Now, Walter, use lots of imagination when you eat these green circles."

Once more Walter's mouth opened to receive the offering, and I could see the hope in his eyes. There was more caution this time, but he was willing to try again. He began to chew deliberately, then looked up at me with a resigned look.

"Are they good, Walter?"

"They're better," he said. He took a few more chews. "Still sorta skushy!" He chewed some more, then concluded, "Granddaddy, this takes a *lot* of imagination!"

Now isn't that just right? We have to face reality and not let anyone fool us with advertisements and slogans, but there are times when we just have to make the best of things. If we use a lot of imagination, and try to make it fun, sometimes we can "get it down." Things may not be ideal, but they can be better.

Thank you, Mr. Walter! First you taught me that my attitude can control my response to life. I can say, "It's a flower to me," if I want! Then you reminded me that not everything is a flower, that in reality some things "are still peas," and can be rejected. And now comes the next lesson: if life dishes us up a bowlful of skushy peas, but we have to eat them anyhow, a little imagination may help us turn them into slightly more desirable "green circles" and get them down. As the song says, "A spoonful of sugar helps the medicine go down!"

I hope I can remember this lesson when I have to go mow the lawn on a day I'd rather be having a picnic. Reality? I'd rather be playing, but the grass has to be cut. Maybe with some imagination I can do it in a different pattern each time, finding the best way to arrive at the imagined treasure at the end of my journey, the pot of gold I am seeking! If even old men can avoid cracks in the sidewalk so as not to break their mothers' backs, I guess I can make up some imaginary adventure to get me through a chore.

The other day in the coffee shop I overheard a conversation between two of our village ministers. You can learn a lot from clergy when they are "off the record." Sometimes more than from sermons!

One was complaining about members of his congregation who were driving him crazy! He couldn't light the candles because they might smoke up the ceiling, which would require repainting at great expense. He couldn't remove the candelabra from the sanctuary because they were a memorial gift. But he didn't want to leave them there, unlit, since that would symbolize "Christ, the Light of the world, has gone out! Extinguished! No light here, folks!"

That was not his only complaint; he had others as well. "Would you believe," he said, "the other day I called on a newcomer to invite the family to attend church, and she reprimanded me! This is what she said: 'I resent your horning in on Sundays. You church people have six other days of the week for services but no, you persist in scheduling them on our one day off!' I was so flabbergasted," he continued, "that I just babbled unintelligibly! It was so outrageous that I couldn't even begin to answer that!"

The other minister was chuckling softly, looking at his colleague with a twinkle in his eye. I noticed that he didn't join in the chorus of complaints but seemed to find them amusing.

"And there is one shut-in," the younger minister continued, "who never remembers when I call on her, and then tells everyone that I haven't been there for months!" He subsided with some muttering that I couldn't quite understand, perhaps fortunately, and shook his head in disgust. "You must have things like this happen too," he finally continued. "How do you deal with them?"

The older minister lowered his voice and leaned forward. I leaned forward in my booth too, so that I could hear as well. Shameless eavesdropping, but it was worth it! Neither of them seemed to notice my presence, and I was able to hear his answer.

"Do you think these things would bother you so much, Brother," he asked, "if instead of being a parish minister you were a chaplain in an insane asylum?"

"Of course not!" his friend rejoined. "If I were a chaplain in an insane asylum I would expect craziness. But I'm not; what does that have to do with it?"

"Here's a little trick for you," was the answer. "The next time someone confronts you with an outrageous idea or unreasonable demand, just whisper to yourself, so nobody can hear, 'Today I am a chaplain in an insane asylum!' Then you'll be able to cope."

His young friend laughed. "I'll try it," he said.

"Don't ever tell," his counselor advised, "or you'll be in bigger trouble. But it works!"

"I can use that at work too!" I thought. Sometimes I deal with people that drive me crazy. Next time I'll just pretend they are crazy. It won't take much pretending.

How do you deal with reality? Realistically. But with a little imagination, you can handle it.

Some things, as Walter said, really take a *lot* of imagination! But I'll work at it.

# 4

## *Going Home*

When Walter was two, his parents moved to Tennessee and, of course, Walter had to go too. A sad day for Grandfather!

But when Walter was three, they moved back to Buffalo! Of course they did not live in exactly the same location, but in a different apartment on a different street. Nevertheless, they were home again, close to me, and I was able to renew my frequent visits with my young instructor.

After Walter and his parents had been back for several months, Walter surprised us one day by saying, "I want to go home to Buffalo now!"

"But we *are* home in Buffalo, Walter," his mother reassured him.

Walter was not convinced.

Well, think about it. When he was two they had lived in a certain apartment, on a certain street, with a beloved back yard. Then they went to Tennessee. Now they were back, but it was not the same. This was a different house. It was not the same at all. Walter had been told they were going *back* to Buffalo; of course he assumed they would be going to the same place as before. But this was *not* the same; therefore, it was not Buffalo!

We may smile at this bit of pseudo-logic by a child, but before you smile too broadly, think of the wisdom contained here!

We can never go back! Isn't that so?

When I go to my hometown, I always determine not to go by the old home place. I don't want to see it! My mom and dad and grandma are all dead and gone; the house was sold long ago; the garden has been turned into a lawn; the big white pine has been cut down. I prefer not to see it; I want to remember it as it was!

But invariably, the last day before leaving, I always go. I drive up slowly and park across the street and just look at it for awhile. The front porch is still there, but the green glider is missing. I can see my parents, in my mind's eye, however, at the close of the day, sitting there in the glider, looking out at the cars passing by. Honeysuckle on the fence across the street is so fragrant it fills the air with its perfume. The old dog is curled up at their feet. Grandma is sitting in the rocker off to the side. The limbs of the big maple reach from the edge of the yard where it was planted almost to the banister of the porch. And I can remember jumping up to the limb to see if I could chin myself on it as often as Dad did, and I never could. Some of the railings on the banister are still crooked, and I smile, remembering how my friends and I used to get the swing going so high that it would finally go crooked and bump against them. My dad must have told me a thousand times to be careful, but it was so much fun to pump the swing and make it fly almost straight out on its chains!

The old house is occupied by strangers. My dog no longer comes running down the sidewalk to greet me. The field across the street has been cleared and buildings erected. The honeysuckle is gone. Different neighbors live in nearby houses. We can never go back. It isn't my home anymore. The memories are still there, but I can't go back.

But truthfully, despite my sad reminiscing, I don't want to go back. I really don't want to be a child again. I'm happy with my wife, with my new home, with my grandson Walter! If some fairy godmother were suddenly to appear and offer me the chance to return to those "days of yesteryear," I would say, "No, thank you. I like to remember, but I like my present life too."

The place I used to live was home then, but it isn't home now. Time has changed it, and me. I feel loss, but not really regret. It is part of my life, but I can't go back. And "home" today is not the "home" of my childhood.

Walter is telling us this! This place which you call Buffalo is not the *same* Buffalo I remember! Now that is not to say it cannot be good, but it is clearly not identical with my memories.

Some people never learn this lesson. They always try to go back, to make up for some past wrong, to recover a past era of life. Consider the seventy-year olds who dress or use hair styles like people in their twenties. Think of retired people trying to impress everyone with how important they used to be. Or parents who follow their children, and try to hang onto the old roles.

Give it up! This isn't Buffalo! At least, not the Buffalo I remember. However, it may be *home*! And that's best of all.

# 5

## *That's Nobody*

When Walter was one and a half his sister, Jenna, was born. At first, Walter was elated! He memorized her name the first time he heard it and wanted to go to the hospital to see Mommy and Jenna! It was exciting to have a baby sister.

However, like many new things in life, the initial joy began to fade a little later. Once Jenna and Mommy came home from the hospital, it was obvious that the new sister was going to take lots of attention from everybody that once had been directed his way. Even Granddaddy sometimes seemed to want to hold the baby and talk about the baby, instead of giving 100 percent attention to his grandson! This was not a good situation, at least from Walter's viewpoint, and it needed to be corrected.

One day when I was visiting, I began asking Walter questions to get him talking. This is a silly game, and children must tire of it, but sometimes they humor adults by going along with it.

"Who's this, Walter?" I asked, pointing at his father.

At first Walter just hung his head, not wanting to play, but finally responded, "Daddy."

"And who's this?" I persisted, pointing next at his mother.

"Mommy," he replied, a little more promptly this time. Maybe getting into this game at least would help him regain the

**115**

center of attention. Granddaddy obviously was paying attention to him now, and not to the new competitor in the family!

"Who's this?" Granddaddy kept asking obvious questions. This time he was pointing to himself!

"Granddaddy!" Walter answered, grinning. Granddaddy was being silly and he liked it when they played silly games.

But then Granddaddy had to ruin it. He pointed at his sister, Jenna, and said, "And who's this, Walter?"

Walter didn't want to play that game. Oh no, just as he was forgetting about Jenna and paying attention to me again, as he should, he was looking at her again. The last thing Walter wanted was for Jenna to get back into the center of things. So he simply didn't answer.

But Granddaddy persisted. "Come on, Walter! You know! Who is this?" It was obvious he was not going to drop the subject.

Walter finally answered, emphatically. "That's Nobody!"

It didn't work, but it was a good try.

Maybe it helped Walter deal with the situation. There are times to try to change a relationship, but other times it just helps to say, "That's Nobody!"

When our new neighbor, Mrs. Graham, moved in next door, I thought it would be a friendly thing to do to walk over, get acquainted, and maybe offer to help her unpack, hang pictures, or assist in some way. I saw her out in her driveway right after the moving trucks left, so I strolled over to say, "Hi, I'm your neighbor. Do you have a moment to talk with me?"

"I certainly do!" she blurted. She was a square-jawed, gray-haired lady with the manner and appearance of an Army drill sergeant, or at least my image of how the stereotypical tough sergeant should appear. "I noticed your garbage cans are still sitting in front of your house," she reprimanded me. "I believe the garbage was picked up this morning. Please see to it that they are removed promptly. I bought this house to be in

**116**

a nice neighborhood, and I don't want the street looking like the road to the dump yard!"

As you can imagine, that was not the reaction I had expected from my overture at neighborliness, so I muttered an apology and retreated quickly to my own yard, not forgetting to take the offending garbage cans with me when I went!

I'll admit I shied away from further contacts for awhile, but not happily. It gnawed at me. I was still trying to think of a way to make friends when, upon coming home one evening, my wife Betty informed me that Mrs. Graham had phoned to tell us to keep our dog from barking. Now, all dogs bark, and our golden retriever, Brandy, doesn't bark much at all, compared with other dogs I know, but occasionally she might! Betty said she had promised to try harder to keep the dog quiet.

Just a few days later, however, Betty looked out the kitchen window to see, to her dismay, that Brandy had gotten lose from her rope and had chased a cat up a tree in Mrs. Graham's yard! To make it worse, Mrs. Graham was out there, shouting something at the dog and practically jumping up and down with rage. Betty took her life in her hands, rushed out the door, and retrieved the dog, all the while being subjected to a constant barrage of verbal abuse.

As Betty told me the story, I could see the color come into her cheeks. "I was so upset," she told me, "but also feeling guilty. I had been baking cookies, so I quickly put a dozen or so of them on a plate and hurried back out the door and across the lawn to Mrs. Graham's yard. I said, 'Here's a peace offering, Mrs. Graham! I'm sorry about the dog and we do want to be good neighbors.'"

"That was really kind, Betty," I replied. "You found a way to make a bad situation turn out well."

"Not really," she responded, sadly. "Mrs. Graham told me to take my cookies, and I think you know where she told me to go with them."

I was furious! Nothing can make me angrier than someone being unkind to Betty, and her description of her ill treatment by Mrs. Graham struck me as intolerable. What is the matter with this woman? I said I would go over immediately and have it out with her, but Betty begged me to let it go. "That would make me feel as though you were trying to protect me, and make me feel helpless," she said. "Just forget it."

I decided she was right, but I couldn't forget it! I thought about it almost constantly. At this point I didn't even want to find a way to make friends with our new neighbor; I wanted revenge! I don't like to admit it, even to myself, but I was eager for a confrontation! I couldn't wait for the chance to tell her my opinion of her attitude, her refusal to act neighborly, and her basic character! I practically went into training so I would be ready, imagining every possible scenario and how I would respond with crushing rejoinders! I spent countless hours, and an abundance of mental energy, in preparation for the "showdown day!"

Whenever I worked in our yard, and noticed she was in her's, I tried to catch her eye. I had my speeches prepared; I was so ready! Whenever our dog emitted even one faint bark, I would fantasize her saying, "Keep your dog quiet!"

Then I would reply, "That's right. A noisy dog can be such a nuisance. Almost as bad as an unfriendly neighbor!"

But I never got a chance. She never would look my way. In fact, it seemed that when we both were outside at the same time, she would find a way to work on the far side of her lawn and not near our boundary.

How frustrating!

And then one day, as I stared at her, I suddenly realized, "That's Nobody!"

That's the way to deal with this! Why didn't I realize it earlier?

Oh, I know it is not the perfect solution. In my opinion, Mrs. Graham has a lot of inner anger, not really related to us. She needs help, but she isn't willing to accept any from us. Time has passed, and I no longer have a desire to bring up the old incident. If she ever looks my way, I'll just say "Hello." If she smiles, I'll smile back.  If she ever opens the door to friendship, we'll walk through it.  But as long as she wants to act as though I don't exist, I'll not waste my time thinking about it.  As long as she wants to abuse us, we'll stay out of her way.  And I certainly don't need to let her occupy my thoughts so much of the time!

When I see her, I'll just remember, "There goes old Nobody!"

# 6

## *How to be a Granddaddy*

One day Walter suddenly concentrated upon my beard. Now, it had been there all along, but I guess he was so used to it, it just hadn't grasped his attention. But today it did, and he reached out to feel it with fascination and curiosity.

"Granddaddy, why do you have hair on your face?"

The question amused me, and I answered, chuckling, "Why, Walter, it just grows there! It comes all by itself. When you get older you may grow hair on your chin too. Little boys don't have beards, but granddaddies do!"

Walter rubbed my beard, and gave me an affectionate smile. "Did you grow it so you could be my granddaddy?"

"Sure!" I replied. "I am glad to grow white whiskers to be *your* granddaddy, Walter!"

The explanation satisfied Walter, and it pleases me to think that, for some time to come now, whenever he sees my beard he'll think I grew it just so I could become his granddaddy. Maybe it wasn't an entirely honest answer, but I think it will do for now.

What does one have to do to be a granddaddy? I'm not talking about obvious answers such as live long enough to have grandchildren! I mean to qualify for the role!

I am sure it means relating! It isn't enough just to see a little kid around, you have to see a *person*, and I mean a person who is at least your equal! Somebody to know, to try to understand, to care about. Somebody immensely worthwhile. Not somebody to care for, although that may be important too, but somebody that has something of value to share with you. As you already know from reading this far, Walter is my teacher in philosophy! He knows I take him seriously and like to spend time in conversation with him. I think that helps transform a person from a grandfather into a granddaddy!

Walter's Mom, Linda, and her husband, Mark, are good parents. There is no doubt about the energy and caring they give to their children and the amount of time they spend thinking of ways to help them grow and develop. But early in their parenting I thought they almost overdid it. I was probably wrong, but I couldn't see why they wouldn't occasionally get a baby sitter for Walter and go out alone, just for the good of their own marriage. But they believed it was so important to be with their baby when he cried, and never to leave him in the care of strangers, that they were willing to deny themselves time away. Linda would say, "If a child knows you are there and will meet his needs in the early years, he'll always be more secure later." So she wouldn't leave him, even for a moment.

I tried to remind her that she had had babysitters and still had turned out okay, but maybe she is right. At least her theory seems to be working well in turning out a fine grandson and granddaughter!

Nevertheless, you will understand why I was so honored when I was invited one day to be Walter's baby sitter for an evening. Walter had turned one, and it was Linda's birthday and she and Mark really wanted to go out to dinner alone. "He has been with you so much, Dad," she said, "that I *think* he'll be okay for a couple of hours. But you must promise to call me if he cries."

"Linda," I said, "I have no doubt Walter will cry when you first leave, but he'll quit in two minutes. We have a good time together, and I know he'll be okay  I'll give him 100 percent attention."

"Okay," she said, somewhat dubiously, as she gave me the phone number of the restaurant where they would be. With many a backward glance she put on her coat, and she and her husband started out the door.

Walter and I were seated on the rug, stacking blocks, as they departed. When the door clicked shut, I looked at Walter to see his reaction to this first-time-ever departure by his mom. To my surprise, he was grinning broadly. He looked up at me and said, "Mummy *out the door!*"

I almost think he added, "...at last!"

Mom's departure meant to Walter that now he had more of Granddaddy's attention, with no adult conversation to intervene. And we had a marvelous time! We stacked blocks, pushed little cars down an inclined board to sounds of "Wheee!", played peek-a-boo, read books, and before you could imagine it, the two hours were over and Mark and Linda were back. Suddenly we heard the door open, and the anxious face of his mother peered around the corner. "Is everything okay, Dad?"

I probably wasn't very tactful, but couldn't resist saying, "Oh yes, Linda, he didn't cry even once!" I'm sure she might have preferred to have been missed at least a little bit!

But Walter was less tactful than I. His face suddenly screwed up into a scowl, and the first tears of the evening appeared. Then he said, "No Mummy! More Granddaddy!"

Uh oh! Playtime with Granddaddy is over! Mom is home; bedtime is coming; Granddaddy is leaving. I am not ready for this!

I don't think it hurt Linda's feelings; I think she understood. But it made my day.

What does it take to be a granddaddy? Not necessarily giving a child 100 percent attention all the time. But liking him, having fun with him, enjoying the time together as much as he does . . . all of that is involved. Letting him pull your whiskers and ask funny questions, and maybe even giving silly answers. Becoming a pupil; letting remarks set you to thinking; realizing there can be deeper meanings in simple responses than at first meet the eye.

And that's why I grew my beard, you see. So I could become Walter's granddaddy!

## 7

## *Remembering*

"I have a really good mind," Walter informed me in a matter-of-fact way. "I never forget anything!"

That was interesting news, I thought! Walter must have heard his parents commenting at some point that he had a good mind and seemed to remember a lot, and he incorporated that into his self-identity. But it seemed a little overstated to me.

Walter was six now, and I worried lest he might be outgrowing his wisdom! Self esteem is good, but arrogance is something else. To say that one never forgets, and to speak of one's own abilities, didn't seem wise to me. Maybe this was an occasion for old Granddaddy to be the teacher!

We were sitting in our favorite ice cream parlor as we discussed Walter's mental prowess, eating vanilla ice cream covered with ants. Yes, ants! At least that is what I always told Walter and his sister, Jenna, when we ordered ice cream there. "Let's get it covered with crawly ants!" I would suggest. That always seemed to them to be an excellent suggestion. So we would gleefully order ice cream covered with ants, and the long-suffering waitress would cover the ice cream with the multi-colored sprinkles which looked enough like ants to make this repulsive order fun. At least it was fun for us!

"Well, Walter," I replied, "I am sure you have a good mind and remember lots of what you are told, but nobody remembers everything. All of us forget things from time to time."

"I don't," he rejoined. "I never forget anything."

Where do you go with this conversation? On the one hand, I didn't want to ridicule him or undermine his self confidence in his good mentality. On the other hand, the statement was so absurd as to deserve challenge. But how could I disprove it? I could hardly say, "Walter, surely you can think of something you don't remember?"

Walter, Jenna, and I liked coming to this ice cream parlor. It had large booths with lots of room to lay your coat or jacket on the bench beside you, spread out any papers you might have brought for coloring or working mazes, and spend a while in deep conversation. The workers there never seemed to mind how long you stayed. And, in addition to that, they had ants for your ice cream!

Working mazes had become almost as much fun as the ice cream for Walter. He was pretty good at them, and always wanted me to draw some for him on the back of the placemat. As I would draw a maze he would say, "Do you mind if I watch?" Of course it made it a little easier to work later if you watched it being made, but I didn't mind; it was a game anyway.

So we would come, take off our jackets and place them on the bench, order our ice cream with ants, and work a few mazes! What a great way to spend an afternoon.

On this particular day, after being informed of Walter's amazing record of never forgetting anything, working our mazes, and eating our ice cream, we finally decided it was time to be on our way. We got up, started for the door, and I suddenly realized that Walter did not have his jacket on. Looking back toward our booth, I saw it still lying on the bench where he had been sitting.

"Walter," I said, "I'm still thinking about how you never forget anything. Are you forgetting anything now? Are you ready to go?"

**125**

"No, I am not forgetting anything and I am ready to go, Granddaddy," he said.

"Are you sure?" I asked, pressing the attack. "You are ready to go home?"

Looking at me in a puzzled and somewhat impatient way, he again assured me that all was in order.

We started toward the door; I gave him every opportunity to go back for his jacket, but he did not. Just before leaving the restaurant, I said, "Walter, what is that lying on the bench where we were sitting?"

Walter turned and looked, saw his jacket, and hurried back to pick it up. As he came back to the door he looked at me with an embarrassed but defiant look and assured me, "I didn't forget this; I was going to go back and get it in a minute!"

I laughed out loud. "Walter, Walter!" I said. "It is okay to admit you forgot it for a minute! Everybody does things like that!"

Walter smiled. "And you love me anyhow, don't you Granddaddy?"

You don't have to be perfect to be loved; in fact, being a little bit imperfect makes a person a little more loveable! I gave Walter a big hug and told him I did love him, and I think he won't forget that!

# 8

## *Not My Life*

Oh, horrors! The sign said "Closed Today for Cleaning and Maintenance."

Walter had been looking forward to going to the zoo for a long time, and I had promised to take him today. He had been jumping around in the seat of the car all the way there, talking animatedly about how we were going to see the tigers, and watch the monkeys, and feed the ducks! He could hardly wait. Now I had to tell him what the sign said.

"Oh Walter," I said, "what a disappointment! The zoo is closed today. They are cleaning it and they won't let anybody in. We'll have to come another time."

Walter looked at me with total disbelief and dismay. "But Granddaddy, you promised!" he pleaded. "You said we could go today!"

"I know, I know," I mumbled apologetically. "But I had no idea it would be closed."

"We can go in anyway," he assured me, "and help them clean it up."

"They won't let us, Walter," I explained. "The gate is locked and they really won't let anybody in. The animals like some privacy during the cleaning, I guess."

"It isn't fair," he objected. I could see the moisture in the corner of his eyes, and his lip began to tremble. I was so disappointed to have to disappoint him.

"Walter," I said, "life is that way. Sometimes, no matter how well you plan, things change and you have no control over them. You don't get to do what you want to do, at least not when you planned to do it. That's life!"

Walter glared at me with defiance. I saw him draw a deep breath, swelling his little chest. He lifted his chin and told me most emphatically, "Not my life."

Not much wisdom there, I thought, but I appreciated the fact that he wasn't going to give up easily. Maybe there was some wisdom in not giving in to life's disappointments without a struggle. I remembered the famous old prayer about changing the things we can, accepting the things we can't change, and knowing the difference. Today Walter and I were confronted by a situation we could not change...or could we?

"Walter," I said, "as usually is the case in life, when you don't get to do what you want to do, there are alternatives. Do you know what alternatives are?

"No," he sulked.

"An alternative," I explained, "is when you do something else because you can't do what you had planned. Now, we can go to the zoo another day, but what can we do today instead? I know a farm that has cows; we could go see cows! And I know an old lady that has a cat with baby kittens. We could go see if she is home and would let us see them. Or we could go to the playground and I could push you on the swing! We'll still have fun."

Walter thought that over for a few moments and finally decided the playground might be fun. I assured him the zoo trip was just postponed. Walter was learning a hard lesson, but as I would discover, he was also teaching me one that I could use later.

Walter's persistence in not giving up when he wanted something was a good trait, it seemed to me. Sometimes people accept "no" for an answer too easily and don't fight hard enough for their goals. I remembered a day last spring when I had been at Walter's home and had asked his mom if I could take Walter outside for a walk. It had been raining hard all day but it had finally stopped and the sun had come out. I was sure Walter would like to get outside and go walking and maybe find some wild flowers to pick for a bouquet for his mother.

Linda replied, "Sure, you two can go walking. But Dad, there are some wild raspberries near the fence and he may want to pick and eat them. I'm afraid they are dirty, so if you two want to do that, take a little bucket and bring them in so I can wash them first."

"Okay," I replied, but without paying much attention. I was sure we would be more interested in flowers than berries, but I should have known human nature better than that! Walter had heard this conversation, so of course the idea of picking and eating delicious berries stuck in his mind immediately. But he didn't say anything.

We left the house, walked down the path, and soon came to the fence. Walter immediately rushed to the vine to pick some berries. "Walter," I admonished, "didn't you hear what your Mom said? The berries need to be washed. We didn't bring a bucket; we could go back and get one though. You can't eat then unless they are washed."

Walter thought that over and then patiently assured me, "Granddaddy, they are already washed. The rain washed them!"

I thought about that. I guess they were! "Well," I said, "you may be right about that. God washed them with his rain. You can eat one or two."

Walter grinned, and it turned out he only wanted one or two. I think he felt he had gotten away with something and at the same time convinced his granddaddy that he was right. Correct on both counts.

I was able to apply Walter's wisdom in my own life in an unexpected way some time later. As mentioned earlier in the book, because of my own carelessness I found a ladder slipping out from under my feet and fell with it, breaking my ankle badly. Being hospitalized for a prolonged period while the doctors tried to determine the type of infection, I saw roommates come and go; I stayed. I felt extremely rebellious and angry. I had a lot to do in my life and being a hostage in the hospital was not in my plans. Other people might be invalids, but this was not to be me. "Not my life!" I vowed.

I tried to read the Bible each day to find comfort, but it didn't seem to be doing me much good. I would pray, asking God to heal me, only to get another report from the doctor that they still had not identified the cause of my continuing infection. What a bummer!

When the kindly African American practical nurse came into the room and caught me with my Bible in hand, she was pleased. "That will help," she had said.

Yet it wasn't helping. I was depressed.

I read the one hundred and twenty-third psalm as she suggested. "To thee I lift up my eyes, O thou who art enthroned in the heavens! Behold, as the eyes of servants look to the hand of their master, as the eyes of a maid to the hand of her mistress, so our eyes look to the Lord our God, till he has mercy upon us." That became my prayer day by day.

One day, shortly after praying, I found myself thinking again about the day Walter and I picked raspberries that were "already washed by the rain." We didn't need to wash them; God had already done it. Then the thought came, "and you have already received God's mercy. God is with you, even here, even now."

With tears in my eyes. I said, "O God, you've already given me your mercy. I want to be well, but I know you are with me no matter what." I felt more peace than I had previously found.

My attitude toward my enforced captivity also began to change. Rather than insisting this is "not my life," I began to look for alternatives. I hardly can say I am glad to look for alternatives. I hardly can say I am glad I was there, but I met some delightful people, had some interesting conversations, and even the adventures that I related earlier in this book. These were not what I had planned to do with my life, but they were alternatives then and memories now. "We know that in everything God works for good with those who love him..."(Romans 8:28 RSV), and I found God could help me even in this situation once my attitude changed.

Once I could say, "I've already been washed by the rain of God's mercy," and "I can find alternatives for how I spend my time today," I no longer needed to insist defiantly, "Not my life!"

Thank you, Lord.